Operation Dinner

How to Plan, Shop and Prep
For Easy Family Meals

Lori Loomis

Dedication:
To my husband.

CONTENTS

Bringing Dinner Back

There is something about the experience of lingering over a shared meal that anchors a family. It's a welcomed interlude to the demands and stress of ordinary life. The unplanned conversations and occasional belly laughs resulting from thirty minutes together around a table gives us a much needed recharging. It washes away the troubles of the world and reminds us what's important. It's a beautiful thing. But all too often it gets lost in the shuffle of long to-do lists and busy schedules of modern day life.

If this has happened to you, then welcome the club.

In my early years as a mom, I found myself overwhelmed and looking for corners to cut. Family meals were one of the first casualties of my over-busy schedule. We would often eat on-the-go, or eat individually as our schedules permitted. At first, I told myself it was a small sacrifice which would happen only for a season while I got a handle on my ever mounting self-imposed list of obligations. But as the days passed, this precious opportunity for family bonding became more and more infrequent.

As this happened, I noticed an increasing distance among family members. I knew that bringing family dinners back would restrengthen the bonds that were fraying and encourage us to spend more time together. So I set about looking for ways to reverse our fragmented mealtimes for good. It wasn't easy. But in my heart I knew it had to be done.

Part of the problem had been my lack of organization and planning in this area, so this is what I tackled first. I set about experimenting. I tested recipes. I tweaked meal plans. Finally after much trial-and-error, I created a system that accomplished the goal of simplifying dinner and getting us all back around the table.

I begin by strategically choosing recipes that share similar prep work, so my time in the kitchen is lessened. At the grocery store, I maximize my time (and money) by doing the bulk of my shopping on a monthly basis. Then I prep enough food for 30 days' worth of meals.

With these techniques along with a few others you will read about later, you'll be able to bring family dinner back just like I did. I'm not talking about sad, soggy frozen meals, either. And it won't require an entire weekend on your feet in the kitchen to accomplish it all. Just a few small changes to yield big results.

Ten Tips for Stress Free Dinner

If your dinner routine needs a little help, then think of this as your quick start guide. Implement these ten steps, and you'll be able to make easy work of dinner every single night.

1. Have a meal plan

If you've never used a meal plan, you'll be surprised how much time and effort you will save. For starters, you'll spend fewer hours in the grocery store, which is always a plus. You'll also save money by avoiding last-minute take-out meals, and oodles of time by having everything prepped in advance. You can set up your plan with some built-in flexibility, so if you need to swap meals around now and again, it's not a problem.

2. Shop Strategically

If at all possible, do the majority of your shopping in one big monthly trip, with a few quick follow up trips for fresh produce and dairy later in the month. This little trick will save you time and money, and will equip you to follow your meal plan to the letter. Here's a bonus: shopping monthly means fewer trips to the store, which in turn means fewer opportunities to spend!

3. Begin the night before

Establish a habit of spending a few minutes in the evening prepping for dinner the next day. Pull meat from the freezer. Get your recipe and ingredients out. Give yourself every advantage you can so that the dinner hour is as simple as possible.

4. Get your family on board
Depending on ages, you can delegate some responsibilities to your children. They can help with measuring and mixing ingredients, or perhaps with the shopping. Older children can even help with putting together a meal plan that includes proper portions of each food group.

5. Prep foods ahead
Most recipes have aspects which can be done in advance. Learn how to spot them in a recipe and how to properly prepare it ahead. For example, if beef stew is on your menu plan, you can take a few minutes after arriving home from the grocery store and cut your beef into bite sized pieces. Since you are doing the bulk of your shopping monthly, do this all at once for several meals.

6. Fill your pantry with easy homemade mixes
Making your own mixes means having the benefit of cost savings along with peace of mind knowing exactly what you are feeding your family. No extra ingredients you can't pronounce. Plus you'll be surprised how much tastier the homemade versions are.

7. Make full use of your slow cooker
Throw in the makings for some homemade applesauce, hot cocoa or a simple soup or sauce to go with dinner. I especially love to use it on the weekend when we're most tempted to go out and eat.

8. Have a well organized kitchen
Having a well-organized kitchen makes for a happy and successful dinner hour. Get your kitchen running like a fine tuned machine, and do a quick inventory to ensure you have all the essential tools to rock this dinner thing.

9. Keep favorite recipes in one central location

In chapter one, we'll cover the basics for making your own meal planning binder. You can gather up your favorite recipes and keep them in one central location, along with meal planning forms, grocery shopping lists and other essential information.

10. Cut yourself some slack

Establishing new habits can be a challenge. You may fall off the wagon a day or two in the beginning. Keep at it. Once you have these tools in place they will reward you with years of family memories around the dinner table, with fewer hassles and headaches

Part 1: The Basics

Chapter 1

Meal Planning Techniques

A meal plan is a useful tool for creating a consistent routine in your household. It will help you save time and money by eliminating extra trips to the store, convenience foods and take-out dinners. Done properly, it will also result in more balanced meals and a healthier lifestyle.

Meal Planning Systems

If you've been unsuccessful with meal planning attempts in the past, it may be time to reevaluate the system you are using. For some individuals, it is important to have a plan with every single detail accounted for. Others may require some degree of flexibility in order to achieve success. Think about your lifestyle, and choose a system that will work best for you.

Have a look at the methods described in the following pages and choose one that suits you best. Your goal is to choose 8-15 recipes which will be used 2-4 times each for a total of 20-31 dinners in a given month. You can allow for some dining out or leftover days if you wish.

> **TIP:** *If you've never made a monthly meal plan, this may seem like a lot of effort at first. But as with anything new, it will get easier and easier the more you do it. So be encouraged and stick with it!*

Option 1: The Precise Meal Plan

This system involves choosing specific meals for every day of the month using a monthly calendar as a tool to keep track of your plan. If you are happiest having every detail planned out in advance, then this is the system for you. The trade-off is that there is less wiggle room for changing things later on.

Choose Your Recipes

1. Select 8-15 of your favorite recipes.
2. Decide how many times you will make each one. In all, you'll want a total of 28-31 meals. For example, if you select 15 recipes you can make each one twice, for a total of 30 meals.
3. Round out the plan by including proper portions of vegetables, fruits, grains and dairy.

Choose recipes with similar prep work whenever possible. As an example, your month could include California Chicken Alfredo (page 69) served three nights, and Bourbon Chicken (page 70) three nights for a total of six meals. Since both recipes require chicken breast diced into 1" pieces, you can do the prep work for six meals at once, then store in the freezer in meal size portions. How easy is that?

Choose Your Sides

Keep your meal plan as do-able as possible by sticking with clean and simple side dishes. Avoid the sauces, syrups and sodium and opt for simple and fresh fruits and veggies. You can make your selections based on what is in season, what is on sale, and/or what looks good. For the grains of your meal, consider making your own breads and rolls. A bread machine will make easy work of this task.

> **TIP:** *Don't forget to consider family outings and special events that may alter your dinner plans when creating your menu.*

Write Your Plan

For the Precise Plan, use a blank monthly calendar to write down the meals and side dishes for each day of the month. Here is an example of a plan consisting of 29 dinners made from 14 different recipes.

Cooked Ground Beef (11 meals):

(4) Baked Ziti, (4) Tex-Mex Soup, (1) Chili, (2) Calzones

Chopped Chicken Breast (6 meals):
(2) Chicken Stir Fry, (3) Bourbon Chicken, (1) Chicken Alfredo

Shredded Chicken (3 meals):
(2) Chicken Tacos & (1) Chicken Enchilada

Beef Roast (2 meals):
(1) French Dip & (1) Leftover Roast Soup

Other (7 meals):
(3) BBQ Chicken
(1) Big Salad
(3) Beef Stir-Fry

This plan would be transferred to a monthly calendar, with each meal assigned a specific day. You can prep this menu by cooking ground beef for 11 meals, dicing uncooked chicken breast for 6 meals and cooking/shredding whole chicken for 3 meals. When the work is done, store them in meal size portions in the freezer, and don't forget to label. Here's an example of a freezer label that includes all the relevant information:

> # Diced Chicken Breast
> ## 11/29/13
> ### *for: Bourbon Chicken*

Prep work is best done on the same day as your monthly shopping trip, so everything is as fresh as possible.

Option 2: The Flexible Meal Plan
For those who need a more flexible option, this system is for you.

Choose Your Recipes
1. Once again, begin by selecting 8-15 of your favorite recipes, choosing those with similar prep work whenever possible.

2. Decide how many times you will make each one, for a total of 28-31 meals.
3. Choose your side dishes.

Write Your Plan

Instead of using a calendar, write your meal plan on a spreadsheet with space for checking off each meal as you serve it.

Flexible Monthly Meal Plan

				Baked Ziti
				Tex-Mex Soup
			▓	BBQ Chicken
	▓	▓	▓	Big Salad
			▓	Beef Broccoli Stir-Fry
		▓	▓	Chicken Stir-Fry
			▓	Bourbon Chicken
		▓	▓	Calzones
	▓	▓	▓	Chili
	▓		▓	Chicken Tacos
	▓	▓	▓	Chicken Alfredo
	▓	▓	▓	Chicken Enchiladas
	▓			French Dip
	▓	▓	▓	Leftover Roast Soup

Begin with a spreadsheet containing four boxes to the left of the recipe name as shown above. Add an "X" or check mark each time you serve one of the meals listed. This allows you to easily see what you have already served and what you have remaining throughout the month.

If there are dishes you don't plan to serve four times, simply shade in the boxes you don't need. In this example, I plan to serve Tex Mex Soup four times, so I have four white boxes. However I plan to serve French Dip only once, so I have shaded in three of the four boxes.

Components of a Healthful Meal

Recently, the USDA replaced the Food Pyramid with a nutritional equivalent shaped as a plate. It gives us a more precise picture of what a balanced meal should look like. The largest portions of the plate are filled with vegetables and grains, while fruit and protein occupy a smaller space. For more details on portion sizes and food groups, visit **www.choosemyplate.gov**.

Source: USDA

See Chapter 7 for information on meal planning with special dietary needs, along with tips for improving nutrition.

The Recipe Rut

We all have our family favorite recipes. The tried and true favorites we turn to when we are pressed for time and need to feed our families. But every so often we may find ourselves in a rut, lacking inspiration for new and interesting meals. If this has happened to you, here are a few ideas for adding variety to your menu.

Use the Sale Ads

Create your meal plan based on weekly sale ads from your local grocery store. Use the veggies and meat you find on sale to inspire meal planning choices.

Collect Family Favorites

Keep track of your best loved recipes in a meal planning binder so you always know where to go for dinner inspiration. There is more on how to create one in the pages to follow.

Theme Nights

Cooking within a specific theme may seem like it would limit your menu options a little. But I've found the opposite to be true. Having a theme as a starting point, I've been inspired to look for new ways to bring it to life. I've managed to find spin-offs and variations that I may have otherwise overlooked.

Nightly Theme Ideas:
- Slow Cooker Meal Night
- Soup & Sandwiches Night
- Pasta Night
- Italian Night
- Mexican Night
- Leftovers/Eat from the Pantry Night
- On The Grill Night
- Chicken Night
- Beef Night
- Stir-Fry Night
- Casserole Night
- Vegetarian Night
- Fish Night
- Pork Night
- Roast Night
- Breakfast for Dinner
- Company's Coming
- Pizza Night

TIP: Make your plan suit your lifestyle. If you enjoy dining out on occasion, write that into the plan! If you need a night or two of easy soup-and-sandwich meals, remember to pencil them in.

Make a Meal Planning Book

A meal planning binder is useful for storing and organizing all necessary information to keep your meal plan on track. Use it to hold recipes, meal planning sheets, shopping lists, coupons, sale ads and anything else required to implement your plan.

You Will Need:
- 3 Ring Binder
- Page Protector
- Tab Dividers

Create Your Categories

Use the tab dividers to create the following sections in your binder:

Category #1: Monthly Meal Plan

Keep your current meal plan here, along with extra blank pages for future months. You can even store past meal plans to reuse over and over.

Category #2: Favorite Dinner Recipes

Store your best loved dinner recipes in this section. Organizing by main ingredient will help facilitate your monthly planning. You can find page protectors of various sizes at your local office supply store that work for organizing index card size recipes, magazine cutouts, as well as full size pages.

Category #3: Shopping List

Store blank copies of your grocery shopping list in this section. The next chapter gives details on how to create one.

Category #4: Freezer, Refrigerator and Pantry Inventory

Use this section to keep track of quantities you have on hand for your most frequently used food items. Here's how to create one:

- Using a spreadsheet, write down 20-30 items you buy most often, including frozen, refrigerated and pantry items.
- Next, do a quick count of how many of each you have on hand.
- Keep it updated with current quantities, and refer to it before making your shopping list.

This will help you avoid overbuying, and possibly wasting food. It will also help to keep your freezer organized by giving you an accurate count of current inventory. Having adequate freezer space is critically important for monthly meal prepping.

Category #5: Coupons and Store Sale Ads

Create a section for compiling and organizing weekly sale ads and coupons.

Assemble Your Binder

Gather the required materials and several of your favorite recipes. Be sure to leave plenty of space for adding more recipes in the future. Set up your binder with most frequently used sections toward the front. I recommend having your meal plan and recipe section in the front, since you will refer to them on a daily basis. Then add inventory checklists, sale ads and coupons in any order. Keep your binder in a central location in your kitchen.

Free Printable Meal Planning Binder Sheets

Get the following printable pages from www.tinyurl.com/mpbinder
- Precise Meal Planner printable
- Flexible Meal Planner printable
- Shopping List printable
- Inventory Checklist printable
- Title Pages for binder

Chapter 2

Shopping

Making a meal plan is only the beginning of our quest to simplify dinner. Next we turn our attention to the importance of gathering the materials needed to implement our plan.

Having a solid shopping plan is an often overlooked but critically important component for success. As with meal planning, this is not a one-size-fits-all activity. For some families, shopping weekly or bi-weekly makes more sense with their lifestyle. For others, monthly shopping is a feasible option. In my experience, the greatest long-term meal planning success is achieved with a monthly shopping system, coupled with quick weekly follow-up trips to replenish perishable items. In this chapter, we will discuss all options.

Monthly Shopping

Committing yourself to once-a-month shopping will take your time saving efforts to the next level. With your new meal plan as a starting point, you'll be able to shop and prep foods for the entire month in one afternoon! That means thirty whole days of stress-less dinner. It also means less time wandering around the grocery store aisles (which means fewer opportunities to spend).

Monthly Shopping: What Should I Buy?

Using your monthly meal plan and recipes, create a shopping list which includes items with a shelf life of 30 days or more. Examples:

- Frozen foods
- Freezable items such as meat, some fresh vegetables/fruit, bread
- Canned goods & shelf stable bottles.
- Baking items such as flour, sugar, chocolate chips, vanilla, seasonings, syrups, etc.
- Dried pasta

Monthly Shopping Step-by-Step

1: Gather Your Materials

You will need a completed monthly meal plan, a blank shopping list and the recipes you selected for the entire month.

2: Begin With Week One

Start by listing ingredients you need for the first week of meals in the appropriate categories on your shopping list. Plan on purchasing all items for week 1, including perishables.

3: List Remaining Ingredients

Proceed with meals for the remaining 3 weeks. List items that can be purchased one month in advance, such as canned goods, freezer items, etc. You will pick up the perishable items for these meals during one of your weekly follow-up trips.

Weekly Follow-Up Trips

With these items tucked away in your pantry and freezer every month, the remaining weekly trips should consist of perishables only. Use your meal plan and create a short list of fruits, vegetables and dairy products. You'll be able to breeze through the dairy and produce sections and be done in just a few minutes. The trick is to avoid the middle aisles and any impulse purchases. Stick to the plan.

For these quick shopping trips, return to your meal planning binder and retrieve the recipes you will be using for the upcoming week. You should already have your main ingredients prepped and ready in the freezer, along with a pantry full of canned and shelf-stable items you need for these meals. Your shopping list should consist of produce, dairy and perishable items only.

Do I Have Enough Freezer Space?

This is a common concern among new monthly shoppers. While its true monthly prepping will use a fair amount of freezer space, with a little organization and planning, it can be accomplished with room to spare. When you consider the benefits of having a viable meal plan for 30 whole days, the effort is well worth it. Here are some strategies for maximizing your freezer space.

1. **Clean It Out** – Rid yourself of any outdated or undesired items first, so you can begin with a clean slate. Then make a habit of doing a quick freezer clean-out every month around meal planning time so you can keep your space organized and clutter-free.

2. **Buy Less Prepackaged Food** – The large boxes and bags of convenience foods can take up valuable freezer space. To say nothing of the undesirable fat, calorie and preservative contents. Consider limiting or eliminating them from your shopping list. As you begin implementing your meal plan, you may find these items are no longer necessary, anyway.

3. **Minimize Packaging** – Be mindful of over-sized packaging used with some frozen foods. When possible, eliminate unnecessary outer boxes, and repackage items in smaller containers or bags as soon as you arrive home from the store to save space.

4. **Choose Appropriate Containers** - When freezing homemade items, choose containers that are the appropriate size so you don't lose space to a partially empty container.

5. **Freeze It Flat** – If you are using large freezer bags for meal prepping, try to make the contents as flat as possible. Otherwise you will lose unnecessary space with irregularly shaped packages that don't stack well.

10 Tips for a Successful Monthly Shopping Trip:

1) Shop when the store is least busy. Early morning or late evening usually works best.
2) Wear comfy shoes.
3) Keep to the list. Avoid impulse purchases by limiting yourself only to things you planned on buying.
4) Bring a buddy, especially if you have a large family and may require a second cart.
5) If at all possible, leave the kids at home.
6) Organize your refrigerator and pantry before you leave. This will cut down on the time it takes to put groceries away.
7) Be prepared to prep some of your foods immediately when you are finished shopping. More on that later.
8) Know your stores coupon policy and bring a copy with you if you can.
9) Eat before you leave. If you've ever shopped hungry, then you know why this one made the list.
10) Make sure the car is empty so you have plenty of room for your haul.

Weekly or Bi-Weekly Shopping

Monthly shopping requires a greater up-front investment of time and money than the typical weekly trips. If you prefer to shop more often, you can still benefit from planning your meals on a monthly basis. Begin by formulating your monthly meal plan as usual. When shopping day arrives, retrieve it from your meal planning binder and use it to compose your shopping list. Then repeat this process weekly or biweekly as needed. If possible, purchase all main ingredients required for the next 2-4 weeks, so you can prep them all at once. This will help to maximize your time for the remainder of the month.

Turning a Meal Plan Into a Shopping List

Now that we have decided on a meal planning system and shopping schedule, we turn our attention to creating a template for writing our shopping lists. The template will consist of categories that we will use to list the items we need for our shopping trips. It will be used over and over again each time we shop. Use the layout of your store as the basis for the categories, or any other method that works for you. The important thing is to find a way to divide up the list to facilitate a quick and easy trip. You can get a free printable shopping list from www.tinyurl.com/mpbinder

Suggested Categories:
- Baking
- Beverage
- Bread/Cereal
- Boxed/Canned Goods
- Dairy
- Frozen
- Household
- Meat
- Personal/Health Care
- Produce
- Snacks
- Other

TIP: Some grocery stores offer a map listing items found in each aisle. With this tool, you can opt to create a shopping list using aisle numbers instead of categories.

Chapter 3

Dinner Prep

You've got your monthly meal plan. Your shopping strategies are in place. Now it's time to learn a few basics to get you on your way toward a successful dinner routine. In this chapter we will cover:

- Dinner Prep Basics
- Organizing Your Kitchen
- Equipment You Will Need
- Freezer Basics

What is Dinner Prep?

Dinner prep consists of selecting certain elements of a recipe to prepare in advance. It's an easy way to lessen the workload of dinner. Let's face it. Everyone wants to save time in the kitchen. But we also want to have delicious and enjoyable meals. Dinner prepping is all about finding a balance between the two.

Dissecting the Recipe

It's time to start looking at your favorite recipes in a new way. Examine them in an effort to find steps that can be done in advance. If you're wondering where to start, a simple stroll through the grocery store will reveal a myriad of ideas. Countless manufacturers have cashed in on our need for convenience by prepping parts of our meal for us. In many instances, if they can do it, so can we.

For example, the frozen foods department is brimming with prepped items such as precooked chicken breast strips, precooked meatballs, chopped frozen vegetables, hamburger patties, dinner rolls, cookie dough and pie crust. In other aisles you'll find pasta sauce, seasoning packets, mixes, applesauce and a huge variety of soups. With the right recipes you can have the convenience of these premade items without the additives, preservatives and hefty price tags found at the store. In other words, you can have the convenience of premade, but in a healthier, more affordable version.

15 Easy Dinner Prep Ideas

1. Make and freeze hamburger patties (page 31).
2. Make meatballs ahead and freeze. (page 33-34).
3. Cook ground beef ahead and freeze. (page 35-36).
4. Prep fresh, uncooked steak by cutting according to recipe instructions and freeze in meal size portions (page 37).
5. Prep affordable cuts of beef such as chuck steak and roast by cutting uncooked meat according to recipe instructions and freezing in meal size portions. Thaw and cook as usual on the day you are serving. (page 38).
6. Cook a whole chicken and shred, then store in meal size containers for future meals (page 54-55).
7. Cut uncooked chicken breast ahead according to recipe instructions (page 56).
8. Prepare pulled pork and freeze in meal size portions (page 80).
9. Dice your own ham for easy casseroles, sides and breakfasts (page 77).
10. Bacon can be cooked ahead and stored in the freezer (page 77).
11. Ground sausage can be cooked ahead (page 78).
12. Buy in-season vegetables, then prep and freeze them (page 101).
13. Buy fruit in-season, then prep and freeze (page 103).
14. Make your own mixes and sauces (page 131).
15. Use your slow cooker more often (page 111).

A Well-Organized Kitchen

A well organized and properly outfitted kitchen makes for a happy cook. It also makes dinner prep run like clockwork. Here are some strategies for organizing your kitchen to improve efficiency.

Declutter

If you're shuffling through drawers to find every tool you need, you'll only end up frustrated and wasting valuable time. A key component to efficient meal preparation is having exactly what you need, where you need it. So begin by clearing out the clutter in your drawers and cabinets.

First, get rid of any broken or duplicate items, or things you do not use. It helps to have a box handy for items to be donated, and a bag for garbage. Weed out items that are used only occasionally and store them in an out-of-the-way place.

TIP: Not sure what you use regularly? Try removing all items you are uncertain about and placing them in a box for the next 30 days. When you need one, use it and return it to its rightful spot in the kitchen.

Evaluate Your Space

Make sure your kitchen layout compliments the needs and lifestyle of your family. For example, if you have small children, consider putting cups and plates in a lower cabinet to encourage independence. Items that are needed at the stove, such as hotpads and cooking utensils should be within arms reach of it. You may find it helpful to make a rough sketch of your kitchen layout and list the desired location for everything as you go. If you find yourself stumped for ideas, a simple internet search will offer a variety of kitchen inspiration.

Spend some time thinking about how you use your kitchen, and how you could make it more suitable to your needs. If you're a coffee lover, create a coffee station complete with coffeepot, filters, mugs, creamers and sweeteners. Similarly, you can create a baking station with pans, mixer and all the necessary tools in one general area. If you have school age children consider an area for lunch prepping, with storage containers/bags and snack items.

To facilitate dinner prepping days, you can designate a drawer or cabinet space for materials such as containers/bags, a permanent marker, labels, meal planning binder,etc. Knives and kitchen tools should be nearby as well. In my kitchen I use the counter space between my sink and stove as the dinner prep area. It's perfect, because it puts me near the sink for washing, and near the stove for cooking. I also have spices, pots, pans, cutting boards and tools in the cabinets and drawers in this area.

TIP: If you have school age children, you can save time by prepping school lunches at the start of every week. Bag cookies, granola, chips and other snack food. This is a project the kids could help with while you do your once a month prep!

Time to Get Moving

Now that you have given some thought to how your kitchen should function, it's time to get to work. Begin by organizing the areas requiring the least amount of change. For example, if you've decided to keep your pots and pans where they are, simply spend a few minutes tidying up, remove any items that don't belong, then move on to your next area. Continue in this fashion until you have worked your way around the room.

Do You Have What You Need?

A smooth running kitchen is aided by a proper set of cooking tools. Here is a list of the most basic essentials.

Knives:	Other Tools:
3 ½" Paring Knife	Whisk
8" Bread Knife	Ladle
8" Heavy Chef's Knife	Spatula
	Grater
Pots & Pans:	Vegetable Peeler
9x13" Pan	Slotted Spoon
9" Round Pan	Cooking Spoon
Jelly Roll Pan	Tongs
Cookie Sheet	Strainer
Pizza Pan or Stone	Masher
Pie Dish	Rubber or Silicone Bowl Scraper
Saucepans with lids	Pizza Cutter
Frypan	Measuring Cups & Spoons
Saute Pan	Rolling Pin
Cast Iron Skillet	Ice Cream Scoops
Dutch Oven	Mixing Bowls, various sizes
Roasting Pan	Cooking Thermometer
	Slow Cooker

This is not a comprehensive list, but covers most basic kitchen needs. Your cooking and baking preferences will determine the remaining items you need.

Freezer Basics

Our modern frost-free refrigerators act by removing moisture from the air, but they'll do the same to ill-packaged foods. Protect your food investment with a basic understanding of proper freezing methods.

Nine Tips for Freezer Success

1. **Grocery Store Packaging is Not Intended for the Freezer**
   Unless of course, it came from the frozen food aisle. For example, pre-packaged ground beef from the meat department was wrapped adequately for refrigeration. If you plan to freeze, you'll need to rewrap in freezer-specific packaging to protect your investment.

2. **Air Is Your Enemy**
   Avoid freezer burn by removing as much air as possible from bags and containers. The exception to this rule is freezing soups, stews and liquids.

3. **Leave Headroom**
   When freezing liquids, remember to leave at least one inch headroom at the top of the container to allow for expansion as it freezes.

4. **Cool Thoroughly Before Freezing**
   When cooking ahead, allow food to cool before freezing. When food is hot, condensation will form on the inside of your container and possibly contribute to freezer burn. It will also raise the temperature of your freezer, and possibly compromise other foods.

5. **Freeze in Small Portions to Preserve Flavor**
   Food that freezes fast retains the best flavor. So freezing in small portions will help accomplish this. Remember never to stack packages of unfrozen food together in the freezer. While they're in the process of freezing, it's important to space them out.

6. **Fresh is Important**
   Freshness and quality of food at the time of freezing will affect the condition and flavor of frozen food. Be sure to buy items at the peak of freshness and freeze immediately.

7. **Flash Freezing**
   With small or delicate items that may tend to stick together when frozen, flash freezing is a great solution. Arrange items on a cookie sheet or freezer safe platter in a single layer. Place in the freezer for 30-90 minutes or until frozen. Then transfer to a freezer bag for storage. This technique works well for freezing berries or individual scoops of cookie dough.

8. **No Aluminum Foil**
   Acidic foods may taste bitter or metallic when aluminum foil is used. It may also undergo color changes, and the foil may begin to corrode.

9. **Thawing Frozen Foods**
   Do not thaw foods at room temperature. Portions of the food that thaw first can breed bacteria. Always be on the safe side by defrosting in the refrigerator.

From Freezer Directly to Slow Cooker: Is It Safe?
In a word, no. The already low-and-slow temperature is reduced even further by the frozen food, producing a temperature ideal for bacterial growth. Always thaw your meat before slow cooking it.

Containers and Packages for the Freezer

Look for containers, wraps and bags that are specifically made for the freezer, and remember to label everything.

- **Heavy Duty Plastic Bags** – Great for just about any freezable item.
- **Aluminum Foil** – As mentioned above, aluminum foil is not recommended for direct contact with some foods. However, you

can use the heavy duty variety as a secondary wrap over plastic for extra protection.

- **Plastic Containers** – Ordinarily these are brittle in cold temperatures, so look for labels indicating they are freezer safe before purchasing.
- **Glass** – Most canning jars will work for freezing, along with other containers made for this purpose.
- **Vacuum Packaging** – These systems provide a reliable way to protect flavor and avoid freezer burn. Price and quality can vary, so be sure to shop around and read reviews.

A Word About Marinade

Avoid freezing raw meat in a marinade. Any marinade containing acidic ingredients, alcohol or salt will chemically "cook" or denature the meat, making it chewy or unpleasant in texture. The best practice is to marinate according to the designated time on the recipe, and always in the refrigerator.

Other Marinating Tips:

- Never marinate in a metal bowl. The acidic liquid can react with the metal for unpleasant results.
- Always marinate in the refrigerator. Room temperature marinating encourages bacterial growth.
- Marinade used with raw meat should not be poured over cooked meat. Potentially harmful bacteria contained in raw meat will carry over. Instead, make a little extra and keep it in a separate container for use on the cooked meat only.
- Rule of thumb: 1/2 cup of marinade per pound of meat.

Part 2: The Food

Chapter 4

Beef

In this chapter we'll cover all things beef. Learn how to choose the correct cut for your recip, how to interpret the labels, as well as a few prepping techniques and easy dinner recipes.

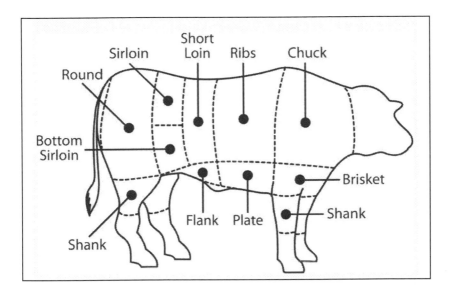

Figure 4.1

Beef Basics

There two main qualities which account for the natural toughness or tenderness of meat: connective tissue and marbling. In a nutshell, connective tissues causes meat to be tough, while marbling makes it tender. A basic knowledge of these qualities will help you choose the right cuts for your recipes, along with the proper cooking techniques for each.

Connective Tissue

Muscles that are used by the animal for movement tend to contain the most connective tissue, which makes them the least tender. Cuts near the shoulder or leg are used most often by the animal, so they will be tougher. A rule of thumb: generally the cuts furthest away from the hoof or the horn will be the most tender. Less tender cuts can also be very flavorful, but proper cooking technique is required.

Marbling

Marbling refers to the streaks and specks of intramuscular fat throughout the meat. When it cooks, the fat melts, resulting in tenderization. The best marbling content with the least connective tissue can be found in the center of the animal. In figure 4.1, you'll notice the rib, short loin and sirloin sections fit this description.

> **TIP:** Most butchers will prepare your order trimmed and portioned to your request. They can debone, butterfly, cut it into strips or pound it out. Be sure to ask!

Cooking Methods for Beef

There are two methods for cooking meat: dry heat and wet heat. Use dry heat for tender cuts and wet heat for tough cuts.

Dry Heat

Dry heat refers to cooking methods that do not use liquid or lids/coverings. It is used for cuts of meat that are inherently more tender, or those that have been tenderized (eg: ground beef or tenderized steak). Examples:
- Grilling
- Broiling
- Sauteing
- Roasting
- Stir-frying
- Deep frying

Wet Heat

Generally a slower cooking method involving liquid. Best for tougher cuts.

- Braising and stewing
- Pot roasting
- Steaming
- Poaching
- Slow cooking

If you have a cut that is full of connective tissue, use any of the following methods to break it down:

- low-and-slow cooking
- braising (cooking in a small amount of liquid)
- cooking fat-side up whenever possible (as in brisket)
- using meat tenderizer
- cutting cooked meat against the grain
- grinding (as in ground beef)

Beef Labeling

Many labels used on meat products are regulated by the USDA and must meet certain standards in order to be used.

All Natural

Meat with this label contain no preservatives or artificial ingredients. The phrase "All Natural" refers only to what is done during and after processing. It is not an indication of how the animal was raised, or whether it was given antibiotics or hormones.

Organic

Organic labels indicate there was no use of growth hormones or antibiotics, and no use of genetically modified feed or animal byproducts. This label does not mean the animal was given a grass-fed diet.

Pasture Finished

Pasture finished animals can still be fed a grain diet, but must have "access" to pasture. Since cattle prefer to eat grain, giving them exposure to pasture does not guarantee they will have much or any grass in their diet.

Grass Fed

This is not a USDA regulated phrase, so there is no verification or standard for using it. But generally, the label means the animal must have access to grass and pasture, and must get most of its diet from grass. A Grass Fed label alone does not guarantee there were no hormones, antibiotics or pesticides.

Dinner Prep: Ground Beef

Ground beef can be useful for prepping in a variety of ways, You can use it to make ground beef patties to be frozen for future use. You can precook and freeze meatballs, or use it to make a variety of easy meals.

Ground Beef Patties

You've probably seen the raw, pre-formed hamburger patties available for a hefty mark-up at your local butcher. Why not do this yourself and have a stash ready to go in the freezer? Form ground beef (or turkey) patties, and stack together with parchment paper between layers. Then place in a freezer safe container or bag and store in the freezer for up to 3-4 months for an easy dinner on those extra-busy nights.

Hamburgers 10 Ways:

Keep your freezer full of hamburger patties, and mix it up with a variety of burger creations:

1. **Burger Cordon Bleu** – Serve with a slice of ham, swiss cheese and a mix of dijon mustard and mayo.
2. **Reuben Burger** – Swiss cheese, thousand island dressing and coleslaw served on marbled rye bread.
3. **Guacamole Burger** – Jalapeno jack cheese, guacamole and shredded lettuce.
4. **Mushroom Swiss Burger** – Melted swiss cheese topped with sauteed mushrooms and onions.
5. **Special Sauce Burger** – Three parts mayo mixed with one part ketchup and one part dill relish makes a great topping.
6. **Italian Burger** – Marinara sauce, mushrooms, mozzarella cheese and a dash of parmesan. This one is great on a big crusty bun.
7. **BLT Deluxe Burger** – Bacon, shredded lettuce and tomato along with sharp cheddar cheese.
8. **Chili Burger** – Cover with your favorite chili, onions and shredded cheddar cheese.

9. **Creole Classic Burger** – Season burger with a dash creole seasoning before cooking. Then combine 1/4cup mayo, 2 teaspoon worcestershire sauce, 1/2 teaspoon hot sauce and 1/2 teaspoon creole seasoning. Serve on burger with jack cheese, lettuce and tomato.

10. **Texan Burger** – Barbecue sauce, jalapeno jack cheese and bacon on texas toast.

Your Favorite Burger Recipes
Your turn. Jot down your favorite ways to make burgers, along with cookbook names and page numbers if applicable. The next time you have a meal planning session, you can use the information listed here to create your shopping list and plan your prep work.

_____

_____

_____

_____

_____

_____

_____

_____

_____

_____

Meatballs

Forget about the precooked meatballs from the frozen foods department.
It's so easy to make your own and have them on hand in the freezer.
They are ten times more tasty than their mass produced cousins, and best
of all, *you* are in control of the ingredients. On page 142 you'll find a
recipe for pasta sauce that goes deliciously with these little balls of joy.

Ingredients:

2 pounds ground beef (or ground turkey)
1 medium onion, chopped
1 cup bread crumbs
1/2 cup parmesan cheese
2 eggs, beaten
1 tablespoon parsley flakes
1 teaspoon italian seasoning
1/2 teaspoon garlic powder

Directions:

1. Combine all ingredients in a large bowl.
2. Roll into 1 – 1 ½" circles.
3. Place on a broiler pan and broil for 2-5 minutes until brown and
   fully cooked. Broiler time will vary by oven so watch carefully.

For Freezing:

Allow to cool thoroughly and store in freezer safe container. Will keep in
the freezer for 3-4 months. When you're ready to use, simply defrost in
the refrigerator overnight.

Meatballs 10 Ways:

1. **Spaghetti and Meatballs** – See page 142 for an easy homemade pasta sauce. Throw them in the slow cooker and cook on low for 2-4 hours or high for 1-2.
2. **Meatball Lasagna** – Prepare your favorite lasagna recipe as usual, with meatballs taking the place of ground beef.
3. **Meatball Stroganoff** –Page 39. Replace ground beef with meatballs.
4. **Meatball Kabobs** – Make an Italian themed kabob with tomatoes, onions, mushrooms and green peppers.
5. **Meatball Stew** – Page 120. Substitute meatballs for stew meat.
6. **Meatball Subs** – A fresh hoagie roll, a little marinara sauce and some mozzarella is all you need. These make great sliders too!
7. **Cheese Ravioli & Meatballs** – Store-bought ravioli and homemade pasta sauce (page 142) makes an easy & filling meal.
8. **Meatball Soup** – Page 117.
9. **Barbecue Meatballs** – Use the freezer-friendly barbecue sauce recipe on page 114. Meatballs and barbecue sauce go in the slow cooker for 3-4 hours on low.
10. **Pepper Meatballs** – Page 48. Replace round steak with meatballs.

Your Favorite Meatball Recipes:
List recipe names and locations here for easy reference when you're meal planning.

All Purpose Cooked Ground Beef

When you're pressed for time, cooking ground beef in advance can be useful. According to the USDA, it can be kept in the refrigerator for 3-4 days or in the freezer for 4 months. It's perfect for adding to casseroles and soups.

Ingredients:

>   3 pounds ground beef (or ground turkey)
>   1 clove garlic, minced
>   1 small onion, diced

Directions:

1. Brown the ground beef with onions and garlic.
2. Drain and allow to cool.
3. Store in freezer safe container or bag in meal size portions for up to 6 months. Remember to label with item name and date.

Ground Beef 10 Ways:

1. **Tacos, Nachos and All Things Tex-Mex** – Page 43. Make enchiladas, taco salad, or your favorite casserole. Lots and lots of possibilities.
2. **Sloppy Joes** –Page 132.
3. **Chili** –Page 119.
4. **Hearty Slow Cooker Tex-Mex Soup** – Page 118.
5. **Cheeseburger Mac** – Add ground beef to the Mac & Cheese recipe on page 123.
6. **Easy Hamburger Soup** –Page 124.
7. **Beef Stroganoff** – Page 39.
8. **Cheeseburger Calzones** – Page 41.
9. **Baked Ziti** – Page 40.
10. **Make-Ahead Coney Sauce** - Page 42.

Your Favorite Ground Beef Recipes

Dinner Prep: Steak

Who can resist a delicious steak grilled to perfection? In our meat-and-potatoes family, it doesn't get much better than that. But if you're looking for something different from the traditional steak and potato, there are some delicious ways to serve it up when you're thinking ahead. Simply cut according to recipe specifications, then freeze in meal size portions for up to 4 months or refrigerate for 1-2 days.

TIP: A Bone-In rib eye is expensive, but you can get a chuck eye steak which is the cut right next to the ribeye for quite a bit less!

Steak 5 Ways:

1. **Stir-Fry** –Page 44.
2. **Kabobs** – Page 45.
3. **Swiss Steak** – Page 46.
4. **Fajitas** – Page 47.
5. **Pepper Steak** - Page 48.

Your Favorite Steak Recipes

Dinner Prep: Chuck

Chuck steak and roast are affordable cuts that can be transformed into a number of delicious meals. Stock up when it's on sale, and cut uncooked meat into meal size portions for up to 4 months or refrigerate for 1-2 days.

Chuck 10 Ways:

1. **Beef Stew** – Page 120.
2. **French Dip** –Page 49.
3. **Carne Guisada** – Page 126. Make tacos, enchiladas, sandwiches and more.
4. **Slow Cooker Pot Roast** –Page 125.
5. **Chili** – Page 119. Substitute chuck steak cut into 1" cubes for ground beef.
6. **Beef Stroganoff** – Page 39. Once again, chuck steak cut into 1" cubes can replace ground beef.
7. **Slow Cooker Beef Barley Soup** – Page 121.
8. **Slow Cooker Beef Burgundy** – Page 122.
9. **Leftover Roast Soup** – Page 50.
10. **Pepper Steak** – Page 48. Chuck steak also works for this recipe.

Your Favorite Roast Recipes

Beef Stroganoff

Ingredients: *Serves 6-8*

1 pound ground beef

2 tablespoons butter

1 cup onions, diced

1 clove garlic, minced

2 (4 oz.) cans mushrooms, drained

1 (10.75 oz.) can cream of mushroom soup (alternative page 133)

1 cup sour cream

6 oz. egg noodles

Directions:

1. In a skillet cook and crumble ground beef until no longer pink. Drain.
2. In a separate skillet, melt 2 tablespoons butter. Add onions, garlic and mushrooms, and cook on medium heat for 3-5 minutes or until onions are translucent.
3. Add cream of mushroom soup and cooked ground beef to onion mixture. Cook and stir for 3-4 minutes or until heated through.
4. Stir in sour cream until heated.
5. Meanwhile, cook noodles according to package directions. Drain.
6. Pour meat mixture over noodles and serve.

Monthly Shopping List	Weekly Shopping List
Ground Beef	Butter
Canned Mushrooms	Onions
Cream of Mushroom Soup	Garlic
Egg Noodles	Sour Cream

Baked Ziti

Ingredients: *Serves 4-6*

1 pound ground beef
1 small onion, chopped
2 cloves garlic, minced
1 (32 oz. jar) pasta sauce (homemade page 142)
1 cup chicken stock (homemade page 113)
1 teaspoon dried oregano
2 cups ziti pasta
2 cups shredded mozzarella cheese
1/2 cup parmesan cheese

Directions:

1. In a skillet, cook ground beef until no longer pink. Add garlic and onion, and cook for another 2-3 minutes. Drain.
2. Add pasta sauce, chicken stock and oregano. Simmer for 7-9 minutes.
3. Meanwhile, cook pasta according to package instructions. Drain.
4. Add noodles to sauce mixture.
5. Pour 1/2 of sauce into a 13"x9" baking dish. Top with 1 cup mozzarella and half of the parmesan.
6. Pour remaining sauce mixture into dish. Top with remaining cheeses.
7. Cover and bake in a preheated 350°F oven for 20 minutes.
8. Remove cover and continue to bake for another 10 minutes or until cheese is slightly brown.

Monthly Shopping List	Weekly Shopping List
Ground Beef	Onions
Pasta Sauce	Garlic
Chicken Stock	Mozzarella Cheese
Oregano	Parmesan Cheese
Ziti Pasta	

Cheeseburger Calzones
Using premade bread dough, this recipe comes together in a snap.

Ingredients: *Serves 4-6*

1 frozen bread dough
1 pound cooked ground beef
4 slices cooked bacon, chopped
2 cups monterey jack cheese
4 oz. cream cheese

Directions:

1. Thaw dough thoroughly and allow to rise.
2. Punch down dough and divide into individual portions.
3. In a bowl, mix together cooked ground beef, bacon, cheese and cream cheese. Spoon into center of dough.
4. Fold dough over to make a pocket. Pinch closed.
5. Bake in a 425°F oven for 14-16 minutes.

Monthly Shopping List
Frozen Bread Dough
Ground Beef
Bacon (if freezing)

Weekly Shopping List
Monterey Jack Cheese
Cream Cheese

Make-Ahead Coney Sauce

Ingredients: *Serves 12-14*

2 pounds ground beef, cooked and drained
2 medium onions, diced
16 oz. tomato sauce
2 cups water
1/4 cup barbecue sauce (homemade page 114)
1/4 cup prepared mustard
1 beef bouillon cube
2 tablespoons dried onion flakes
2 tablespoons chili powder
1 tablespoon sugar
1 teaspoon hot sauce
1 teaspoon garlic powder
1 teaspoon ground cumin

Directions:

1. In a skillet, cook and crumble ground beef. Drain.
2. Combine ground beef and all remaining ingredients in a pot and bring to a boil.
3. Reduce heat, cover and simmer on low for 1-2 hours.
4. Serve over hot dogs, or allow to cool and store in the freezer for up to 3 months.

Monthly Shopping List

		Weekly Shopping List
Ground Beef	Chili Powder	Onions
Tomato Sauce	Sugar	
Barbecue Sauce	Hot Sauce	
Prepared Mustard	Garlic Powder	
Beef Bouillon Cube	Dried Cumin	
Dried Onion Flakes		

Mexican Seasoned Ground Beef

On days when you are super rushed, it's nice to have this meat precooked and ready to go. Pull it from the freezer and use it in enchiladas, nachos, tacos, or casserole.

Ingredients:

> 1 pound ground beef
> 2 tablespoons taco seasoning mix from page 135

Directions:

1. Brown ground beef and drain.
2. Add 2 tablespoons taco seasoning mix and 1/3 cup water.
3. Continue to cook on low for 5-7 minutes.
4. Serve immediately or cool and store in freezer safe container for up to 6 months.

Monthly Shopping List:
All ingredients

Basic Stir-Fry Sauce

When sirloin is on sale, stock up. But instead of just freezing as-is, cut it into 1-2 inch strips and freeze in meal-size containers and label. This sauce is delicious with beef, chicken, pork or shrimp. Add a pinch of red pepper flakes if you like a little kick.

Ingredients:

> 1/3 cup soy sauce
>
> 1 cup chicken stock (homemade page 113)
>
> 1 tablespoon cider vinegar
>
> 1 tablespoon sugar
>
> 1 teaspoon sesame oil
>
> 1/4 teaspoon ground ginger
>
> 1/2 teaspoon garlic powder
>
> 2 tablespoons cornstarch

Directions:

1. Combine all ingredients except cornstarch.
2. Place cornstarch in a separate bowl and gradually pour in the soy sauce mixture. Whisk until combined.
3. Store in refrigerator for 5-7 days or use immediately with your favorite stir-fry ingredients.
4. To use, stir fry your meat and vegetables as desired, adding sauce during the last half of cooking. You'll want to use enough sauce to coat the ingredients without drowning them. Amount you need will vary depending on the size of your meal.

   NOTE: if you plan to make this sauce ahead, be sure to mix well before using, as ingredients will separate.

Monthly Shopping List:
All ingredients

Basic Kabob Marinade

Kabobs are a great use for sirloin or round steak. Just cut into cubes and store in meal size containers in the refrigerator for up to 3 days or in the freezer for up to 6 months. If you like smoked sausage, stock up when It's on sale and slice it into 1/2" – 3/4" pieces. Be sure to freeze it in a separate bag. Now you have all the meat components ready for your next grilling night.

This marinade goes great with beef, chicken and pork. Even great for marinating vegetables! You can make this ahead and store it in the refrigerator for 5-7 days.

Ingredients:

> 1/2 cup soy sauce
>
> 1/2 cup tomato sauce or ketchup
>
> 2 tablespoons sugar
>
> 1 teaspoon garlic powder
>
> 1 teaspoon ginger

Directions:

1. Mix all ingredients together.
2. Use immediately or store in the refrigerator for up to 7 days.
3. To use, cover meat and/or vegetables with this mixture and marinade in the refrigerator for 2-6 hours. Create your kabobs and cook as usual.

> *TIP: On occasions when you have leftover meatballs, why not make an italian-style kabob with tomatoes, onions, green peppers and mushrooms!*

Monthly Shopping List:
All ingredients

Swiss Steak

Purchase a round steak and cut it into serving size portions, then label it and store in the freezer for up to 6 months or the refrigerator for up to 3 days.

Ingredients: *Serves 4-6*

3/4 cup flour
1 teaspoon salt
1/2 teaspoon pepper
1/2 teaspoon garlic powder
2 pounds beef round steak, cut into serving size pieces
2 tablespoons vegetable oil
1 (14.5 oz.) can diced tomatoes
1 cup beef stock (homemade page 112)
1 small onion, sliced

Directions:

1. In a bowl, mix together flour, salt, pepper and garlic powder.
2. Place steak on cutting board and sprinkle flour mixture on both sides. Pound into meat or press with fork.
3. In a large skillet, heat oil and brown steak on both sides.
4. Transfer to casserole dish.
5. Add diced tomatoes (including juices), beef stock and sliced onion.
6. Cover and cook in a 350°F oven for 90 minutes.

Monthly Shopping List		Weekly Shopping List
Beef Round Steak	Garlic Powder	Onion
Flour	Vegetable Oil	
Salt	Diced Tomatoes	
Pepper	Beef Stock	

Fajita Marinade

This recipe works best for 1 lb of beef, pork or chicken.

Ingredients:

1/4 cup olive oil

2 tablespoons lime juice

2 cloves garlic, minced

1 teaspoon chili powder

1 teaspoon cumin

1 teaspoon ground black pepper

1 teaspoon salt

1/4 teaspoon red pepper flakes

Directions:

1. Mix all ingredients together and use as a marinade for fajita meat. Or store in the refrigerator for 2-3 days.

> **TIP:** *Place fresh meat in the freezer for 30 minutes to make it easier to cut.*

Monthly Shopping List:
All ingredients

Pepper Steak

Another easy and filling crowd pleaser that works well for prepping ahead.

Ingredients: *Serves 4-6*

1 ½ pounds beef round steak, cut into 2" strips
2 tablespoons vegetable oil
1 (14.5 oz.) can diced tomatoes
1 cup beef stock (homemade page 112)
1/3 cup soy sauce
1 medium onion, sliced
1 green bell pepper, cut into 1-2" strips
2 cloves garlic, minced
2 teaspoons cornstarch
1/4 cup water

Directions:

1. In a skillet, brown steak strips in vegetable oil.
2. Add diced tomatoes (including juices), beef stock, soy sauce, onion, green pepper and garlic.
3. Cook uncovered on medium-low heat until onions and green peppers are soft.
4. Dissolve cornstarch in water. Slowly stir into skillet. Continue to stir until thickened, about 3 minutes.
5. Serve with rice or noodles.

Monthly Shopping List		Weekly Shopping List
Beef Round Steak	Beef Stock	Onions
Vegetable Oil	Soy Sauce	Green Pepper
Diced Tomatoes	Cornstarch	Garlic

French Dip

Ingredients: *Serves 6-8*

4 pounds boneless chuck roast (or round roast)
1-2 cups fresh mushrooms, sliced
1 cup beef stock (homemade page 112)
1/2 cup balsamic vinegar
2 tablespoons worcestershire sauce
1 tablespoon honey
4 cloves garlic, minced
1/2 teaspoon red pepper flakes
6-8 hoagie buns

Directions:

1. In a bowl, mix together beef stock, balsamic vinegar, worcestershire sauce, honey, garlic and red pepper flakes.
2. Place roast and mushrooms in slow cooker and pour liquid ingredients over.
3. Cook on low for 6-8 hours or until fork tender.
4. Remove from slow cooker and shred with fork.
5. Serve on hoagie rolls. Use liquid from slow cooker for dipping sauce.

Monthly Shopping List		Weekly Shopping List
Boneless Chuck Roast	Honey	Mushrooms
Beef Stock	Red Pepper Flakes	Hoagie Buns
Balsamic Vinegar	Worcestershire Sauce	Garlic

Leftover Roast Soup

No more groans from the peanut gallery when it's time to serve leftovers! This soup is a favorite of even my most picky eater.

Ingredients: *Serves 4-6*

2 cups sliced mushrooms

1 medium onion, chopped

2 stalks celery, chopped

3 cloves garlic, minced

2 tablespoons butter

1 ½ – 2 pounds leftover beef roast, diced

64 oz. beef stock (homemade page 112)

1 tablespoon worcestershire sauce

8 oz. egg noodles

Directions:

1. In a large pot, cook mushrooms, onions, celery and garlic in butter over medium heat until softened.
2. Add remaining ingredients. Bring to a boil.
3. Reduce heat and add egg noodles.
4. Continue to cook for 10-12 minutes, stirring occasionally until noodles are tender.

Monthly Shopping List
Beef Roast
Beef Stock
Worcestershire Sauce
Egg Noodles

Weekly Shopping List
Mushrooms
Onions
Celery
Garlic
Butter

Chapter 5

Chicken

Chicken is a great ingredient for meal planning because it's affordable, relatively foolproof and loved by just about everybody. In this chapter, we'll discuss issues of labeling and safe handling with poultry, along with a variety of easy dinner options.

Chicken Basics: Safety

Raw chicken can contain salmonella and other bacteria that cause food poisoning, so safe handling are important.

- Cook raw chicken within 24-48 hours of purchasing.
- To be on the safe side, add your chicken to the shopping cart right before checkout and refrigerate it as soon as you arrive home.
- Washing raw chicken is not recommended. It can contaminate your sink, faucet and other dishes.
- According to food safety guidelines, chicken must be cooked to an internal temperature of at least 165°F. Test in the thickest part of the breast and the innermost part of the wing and thigh.
- Never leave raw chicken at room temperature, even to defrost.
- Always use as separate cutting board for raw chicken.
- Wash your hands thoroughly after touching raw poultry and before touching anything else.
- Wash all countertops, utensils and anything that comes in contact with raw chicken. Many harmful bacteria cannot survive high temperatures so be sure your water is hot.

TIP: White Meat is leaner and cooks more quickly. Dark meat is more flavorful and works well for stews.

USDA Approved Labels

The following labels are regulated by the USDA. Manufacturers must meet certain standards minimum standards in order to use them.

Organic

Certified organic poultry is prohibited from having any antibiotics at any time. It's important to note there are a few variations within the term organic:

1. "100% Organic" – all ingredients and processing aids are organic.
2. "Organic" – all agricultural ingredients must be certified organic, except where specified on the National List. Non organic ingredients allowed up to a total of five percent.
3. "Made With Organic" – at least 70% of the product must be certified organic.

Free Range or Free Roaming

Chickens labeled as "free range" must be allowed access to the outside during their lifetime. There is no rule about the amount of space they are given, so it may not be an indication of quality of life.

No Antibiotics Administered (or No Antibiotics Added)

With this label you will also normally find an accompanying certification shield from the USDA or private certifier.

Hormone Free

Manufacturers in the U.S. are prohibited by law from using hormones in chicken. So when you see the phrase "hormone free", it does not indicate additional quality steps in raising or processing.

Natural

This label gives no indication of how the bird was raised, It merely tells us nothing has been added to the chicken after slaughter

Other Poultry Labels

Broiler – Chickens that are 6-8 weeks old and weigh around 2.5 pounds.

Fryer – Chickens 6-8 weeks old weighing 2.5 to 3.5 pounds.

Roaster – Less than 8 months old and weighing 3.5 to 5 pounds.

All of these are young chickens raised for their meat, so you can use them interchangeably for any recipe. Just choose the size that fits your needs. If you choose a larger or smaller bird than is called for in a recipe, remember to adjust the cook time.

Dinner Prep: Shredded Chicken

Having shredded chicken on hand allows for a variety of delicious dinner options, including soups, casseroles, sandwiches and lots more!

This recipe calls for two whole chickens, but you can easily double it if you have a large family like mine. You can use the liquid created by this recipe to make some superb chicken stock (page 113) and have the beginnings of an unforgettable soup. Use cooked shredded chicken within 3 days or store in freezer for up to 4 months.

Ingredients:

>   2 whole chickens (3-4 pounds each)
>   4 cloves garlic, coarsely chopped
>   2 tablespoon whole peppercorns
>   1 tablespoon salt
>   2 large onions, coarsely chopped
>   2-3 ribs celery, chopped
>   4-5 carrots, chopped
>   3 bay leaves

Directions:

1. Place all ingredients in large stock pot and cover with water.
2. Cook covered until boiling.
3. Reduce heat to a gentle boil and continue cooking for 1 ½ - 2 hours or until meat is tender and falling off the bone.
4. Remove meat and allow to cool. Freeze in meal size portions.
5. Reserve the liquid and bones in the stockpot and follow the recipe on page 113 to make your own chicken stock.

Shredded Chicken 10 Ways:

Precook and shred chicken, then use it to make a variety of easy meals.

1. **Chicken Bacon Club Sandwiches** –Page 57.
2. **Traditional Chicken Noodle Soup** –Page 58.
3. **White Chicken Chili** – Page 59.
4. **Slow Cooker Spicy Chicken Stew** – Page 127.
5. **The Best Chicken Enchiladas** - Page 60.
6. **Chicken Tacos** – Page 128.
7. **Easy Chicken Pot Pie** – Page 62.
8. **Chicken Wraps with Chipotle Mayo** – Page 63.
9. **Buffalo Chicken Rolls** – Page 64.
10. **Creamy Mexi-Chicken Casserole** – Page 65.

Your Favorite Shredded Chicken Recipes

List the names of your favorite shredded chicken recipes, along with recipe sources (cookbook name, page number, etc.) so you can easily find them when meal planning.

_____

_____

_____

_____

_____

_____

_____

_____

Dinner Prep: Chicken Breast

Prepare your uncooked chicken breast for future meals by slicing into strips or dicing into chunks if necessary, then divide into meal size containers and they'll be ready-to-go in the freezer. Thaw and cook as usual on dinner day.

Chicken Breast 10 Ways:

1. **Chicken Stir Fry** – Page 44.
2. **Chicken Fajitas** –Page 47.
3. **Chicken Kabobs** – Page 45.
4. **Cajun Chicken Pasta** – Page 67.
5. **Chicken Bacon Quesadillas** – Page 68.
6. **California Chicken Alfredo** –Page 69.
7. **Bourbon Chicken** – Page 70.
8. **One Pot Chicken & Veggies** – Page 72.
9. **Simplified Chicken Cordon Bleu** – Page 73.
10. **Easy Kung Pao Chicken** – Page 74.

Your Favorite Chicken Breast Recipes

_____
_____
_____
_____
_____
_____
_____
_____
_____

Chicken Bacon Club Sandwiches

This is sandwich nirvana. A dash of hot sauce gives it a deliciously subtle kick. The chicken mixture also makes a great cracker dip.

Ingredients: *Serves 4-6*

2 cups cooked shredded chicken

1 cup mayonnaise

1/4 cup celery, diced

1 teaspoon chipotle hot sauce

1/8 teaspoon garlic powder

6-10 slices bacon, cooked and drained

whole grain bread, toasted

provolone cheese slices

lettuce

tomato

Directions:

1. Combine first five ingredients.
2. Spread on whole grain toast.
3. Top with cheese, bacon, lettuce and tomato and serve immediately.

Monthly Shopping List	Weekly Shopping List
Chicken	Celery
Mayonnaise	Whole Grain Bread
Chipotle Hot Sauce	Provolone Cheese
Garlic Powder	Lettuce
Bacon (if freezing)	Tomato

Traditional Chicken Noodle Soup

Oh, so easy to make when you have shredded chicken on hand. You'll wonder why you ever bought the canned variety.

Ingredients: *Serves 4-6*

2 tablespoons butter

1 stalk celery, diced

2-3 carrots, diced

1 medium onion, diced

4 (14 oz.) cans chicken stock (homemade page 113)

2 teaspoons chicken bouillon

1 teaspoon poultry seasoning

1 teaspoon thyme

2 cups cooked shredded chicken

1/2 cup heavy cream

4 oz. egg noodles

Directions:

1. In a large pot, melt butter. Cook celery, carrots and onion for 2-3 minutes or until soft.
2. Add chicken stock, bouillon, poultry seasoning and thyme. Bring to a boil.
3. Reduce heat and add shredded chicken, uncooked egg noodles and heavy cream.
4. Cook on low for 15-20 minutes, stirring occasionally.

Monthly Shopping List	Weekly Shopping List
Chicken Stock	Butter
Chicken Bouillon	Celery
Poultry Seasoning	Carrots
Thyme	Onion
Chicken	Heavy Cream
Egg Noodles	

White Chicken Chili

Ingredients: *Serves 4-6*

2 tablespoons butter

1 medium onion, diced

2 cloves garlic, minced

1 (14 oz.) can chicken stock (homemade page 113)

1 ½ cup cooked shredded chicken

2 (15 oz.) cans great northern beans, drained and rinsed

1 (4 oz.) can diced green chiles

1 teaspoon oregano

1 teaspoon fresh ground black pepper

1/4 teaspoon cayenne pepper (optional)

1 cup monterey jack cheese, shredded

1/2 cup heavy cream

Directions:

1. In a pot, melt butter. Cook onion in butter for 2-3 minutes.
2. Add garlic and cook additional 2-3 minutes.
3. Add chicken stock, shredded chicken, beans, green chiles, oregano, black pepper and cayenne pepper.
4. Cook on low for 20-25 minutes.
5. Add Monterey jack cheese and heavy cream. Cook until cheese is thoroughly melted and mixed. Serve immediately.

Monthly Shopping List		Weekly Shopping List
Chicken Stock	Black Pepper	Butter
Chicken	Cayenne Pepper	Onion
Great Northern Beans		Garlic
Diced Green Chiles		Monterey Jack Cheese
Oregano		Heavy Cream

The Best Chicken Enchiladas

Ingredients: *Serves 4-6*

For The Chicken Filling:
> 2 pounds cooked shredded chicken
> 1 (16 oz.) jar salsa
> 1 pkg. taco seasoning mix (homemade page 135)

For The Enchiladas:

> 10-12 enchilada size flour tortillas
> 2 cups shredded monterey jack cheese, divided
> 3 tablespoons butter
> 3 tablespoons flour
> 2 cups chicken stock (homemade page 113)
> 1 cup sour cream
> 1 (4 oz.) can diced green chiles

Directions:

Chicken Filling
> Combine shredded chicken, salsa and taco seasoning in a skillet. Cook covered on low heat for 6-10 minutes. Use immediately for chicken tacos or nachos, or for enchilada recipe below.

Enchiladas
1. Combine shredded chicken mixture with 1 cup cheese.
2. Spoon into tortillas and roll up.
3. Place in a greased 9 x 13" pan.
4. Meanwhile, melt butter in a saucepan.
5. Add flour and cook on medium, stirring constantly until thickened and well combined.
6. Add chicken stock and green chiles, and cook on medium heat, stirring occasionally until sauce is thickened.
7. Remove from heat and stir in sour cream.
8. Pour over enchiladas and top with remaining cheese.

9. Bake uncovered at 350°F for 20-22 minutes, then broil for 2-3 minutes until cheese is lightly browned.

Monthly Shopping List

Chicken

Salsa

Taco Seasoning

Chicken Stock

Diced Green Chiles

Weekly Shopping List

Flour Tortillas

Monterey Jack Cheese

Butter

Flour

Sour Cream

Easy Chicken Pot Pie

Ingredients: *Serves 4-6*

> 1/3 cup butter
>
> 2/3 cup flour
>
> 4 cups heavy cream
>
> 1/4 cup chicken stock (homemade page 113)
>
> 2 cups cooked shredded chicken
>
> 1 tablespoon garlic, minced
>
> 1/2 cup onion, diced
>
> 1 cup diced potatoes
>
> 1/2 cup carrots, diced
>
> 1/2 cup canned or frozen peas
>
> 1 can refrigerator biscuits

Directions:

1. In a saucepan, combine flour and butter, stirring constantly until thickened.
2. Slowly stir in heavy cream and chicken stock. Cook until warmed through.
3. Add chicken, garlic, onion, potatoes, carrots and peas.
4. Cook on med-low, stirring occasionally for 5-7 minutes.
5. Pour into individual ramekins or custard cups.
6. Slice biscuits into thin strips and weave on top of chicken mixture to form top crust.
7. Bake at 350°F for 18-20 minutes.

Monthly Shopping List
Chicken
Flour
Chicken Stock
Canned or Frozen Peas

Weekly Shopping List
Refrigerator Biscuits
Butter
Heavy Cream
Garlic
Onion
Carrots

Chicken Wraps with Chipotle Mayo

Ingredients: *Serves 4-6*

2 cups cooked shredded chicken

4 flatbread wraps

toppings of your choice

Chipotle Mayo:

1/2 cup mayonnaise

1 tablespoon chopped chipotle chili in adobo sauce

1 teaspoon fresh lime juice

Directions:

1. *For the mayo:* Combine mayo, chipotle chili and lime juice in a food processor and process until smooth. Refrigerate for at least 30 minutes to allow flavors to marry.
2. Add chipotle mayo to a flatbread wrap. Top with shredded chicken and your favorite toppings, like lettuce, bacon and tomato!

TIP: *Chipotle mayo will keep in the refrigerator for up to one week. Mix well before serving.*

Monthly Shopping List
Chicken
Mayonnaise
Chipotle Chili in Adobo Sauce

Weekly Shopping List
Flatbread Wrap
Lime
Your Favorite Toppings

Buffalo Chicken Rolls

If you love buffalo chicken wings but hate the fat and calories. Here's a great alternative with all the flavor you could hope for!

Ingredients: *Serves 4-6*

> 1 cup cooked shredded chicken
>
> 12 egg roll wrappers
>
> 1/2 cup hot sauce
>
> 2 oz. cream cheese
>
> 1 cup crumbled blue cheese
>
> 1 cup cabbage, chopped
>
> non-stick cooking spray
>
> blue cheese dressing for dipping

Directions:

1. In a skillet on medium-low heat, mix together chicken, hot sauce and cream cheese until warmed through and well blended.
2. Fill egg roll wrappers by starting at the bottom corner, layering cabbage, chicken mixture and blue cheese.
3. Fold sides in, then roll wrapper to the end.
4. Place egg rolls on a cookie sheet and spray lightly with nonstick cooking spray.
5. Bake at 400°F for 7-9 minutes, then flip and continue cooking for 5-7 minutes or until lightly brown on all sides.

Monthly Shopping List	Weekly Shopping List
Chicken	Egg Roll Wrappers
Hot Sauce	Cream Cheese
Blue Cheese Dressing	Crumbled Blue Cheese
Nonstick Cooking Spray	Cabbage

Creamy Mexi-Chicken Casserole

Ingredients: *Serves 6-8*

    2 tablespoons butter

    1 medium onion, diced

    2 (4 oz.) cans green chiles

    3 1/2 cups cooked shredded chicken

    1 cup chicken stock (homemade page 113)

    1 (10 oz.) bag frozen corn

    1 (10 oz.) can enchilada sauce

    1/4 teaspoon cayenne pepper

    1 cup sour cream

    2 oz. cream cheese

    1 cup monterey jack cheese

    12 corn tortillas

    1 cup sharp cheddar cheese

    tortilla chips

Directions:

1. In a large skillet, melt butter. Cook onions until tender, about 3-4 minutes.
2. Add green chiles, shredded chicken, chicken stock, corn, enchilada sauce, cayenne pepper, sour cream, cream cheese and monterey jack cheese.
3. Cook on medium-low heat for 5-7 minutes or until cooked through.
4. Layer 4 tortillas in the bottom of a greased 13x9" pan.
5. Spoon chicken mixture on top.
6. Repeat layers two more times.
7. Top with cheddar cheese and crushed tortilla chips.
8. Bake at 350°F for 30 minutes.
9. Allow to stand for 10 minutes before serving.

Monthly Shopping List

Green Chiles

Chicken

Chicken Stock

Frozen Corn

Enchilada Sauce

Cayenne Pepper

Weekly Shopping List

Butter

Onion

Sour Cream

Cream Cheese

Monterey Jack Cheese

Corn Tortillas

Sharp Cheddar Cheese

Tortilla Chips

Cajun Chicken Pasta

Ingredients: *Serves 6-8*

12 oz. fettuccini noodles
2 tablespoons olive oil
1 pound boneless, skinless chicken breasts, sliced into 1" strips
2 cloves garlic, minced
2 (14.5-oz.) cans diced tomatoes, drained
1/4 cup chicken stock (homemade page 113)
2 cups heavy cream
1 tablespoon cajun blackening spice
2 cups parmesan cheese, grated

Directions:

1. Cook pasta according to package instructions.
2. Meanwhile in a skillet, heat olive oil. Add chicken and garlic and cook until no longer pink.
3. Add diced tomatoes, chicken stock, heavy cream and cajun spice. Cook on low for 3-4 minutes.
4. Add parmesan cheese and continue to cook on low until cheese is melted and sauce is thickened.
5. Toss chicken mixture with cooked pasta until thoroughly combined. Serve.

Monthly Shopping List
Fettuccini Noodles
Olive Oil
Chicken Breast
Diced Tomatoes
Chicken Stock
Cajun Blackening Spice

Weekly Shopping List
Garlic
Heavy Cream
Parmesan Cheese

Chicken Bacon Quesadillas

Ingredients: *Serves 4-6*

> 1 pound boneless, skinless chicken breast
>
> 10 bacon strips
>
> 1 tablespoon butter
>
> 8 flour tortillas
>
> 1 avocado, diced
>
> 1/4 cup fresh salsa
>
> 8 oz. cheddar or pepper jack cheese

Directions:

1. Cook chicken breast on a grill until cooked through and no longer pink. Cut into strips.
2. Meanwhile, cook bacon until crisp, and crumble.
3. In a skillet, melt butter over medium heat.
4. Add tortilla to hot skillet. Top with grilled chicken strips, crumbled bacon, diced avocado and 1-2 teaspoon fresh salsa.
5. Top with cheese and a second tortilla.
6. Cover and cook until cheese is melted and bottom of tortilla is slightly brown.
7. Flip carefully and cook the other side until slightly brown.
8. Repeat steps until all quesadillas have been made. Cut into quarters and serve.

Monthly Shopping List
Chicken
Bacon (if freezing)

Weekly Shopping List
Butter
Flour Tortillas
Avocado
Fresh Salsa
Cheddar or Pepper Jack Cheese

California Chicken Alfredo

Ingredients: *Serves 6-8*

2 tablespoons olive oil

1 pound chicken breast, cut into 1" cubes

1 clove garlic, minced

8-12 oz. bag frozen california blend vegetables (carrots, broccoli and cauliflower)

2 cups farfalle pasta (bowtie)

1 cup heavy cream

1 cup parmesan cheese

Directions:

1. In a skillet heat olive oil. Add chicken pieces and cook 4-5 minutes on medium heat, stirring occasionally.
2. Add garlic and vegetables. Cover and continue to cook until chicken is no longer pink and vegetables are soft.
3. Meanwhile, cook pasta according to package directions. Drain.
4. Add heavy cream and parmesan to chicken mixture. Cook and stir until thickened and thoroughly blended.
5. Mix with cooked pasta and serve.

Monthly Shopping List
Olive Oil
Chicken Breast
Frozen California Blend Vegetables
Farfalle Pasta

Weekly Shopping List
Garlic
Heavy Cream
Parmesan Cheese

Bourbon Chicken

Ingredients: *Serves 6-8*

2 pounds boneless, skinless chicken breast, cut into 1" cubes
1/4 cup flour
2 tablespoons olive oil
1 clove garlic, minced
1/4 teaspoon powdered ginger
1/2 teaspoon red pepper flakes
1/4 cup apple juice
3 tablespoons light brown sugar
1 teaspoon cider vinegar
1/3 cup soy sauce
1/2 cup plus 1 tablespoon water
1 tablespoon corn starch

Directions:

1. Roll chicken breast in flour, coating thoroughly.
2. In a skillet heat olive oil. Add coated chicken pieces and cook just until lightly brown, about 2 minutes per side.
3. Remove chicken from pan and set aside.
4. To the skillet add garlic, ginger, red pepper flakes, apple juice, light brown sugar, cider vinegar, soy sauce and 1/2 cup water. Cook on low for 4-6 minutes.
5. Return chicken to pan with sauce. Continue to cook on medium-low for 12-15 minutes.
6. In a bowl mix corn starch with 1 tablespoon water. Add to pan and stir until sauce is thickened.
7. Serve over a bed of rice with stir fry veggies or whatever you fancy!

Monthly Shopping List

Chicken Breast

Olive Oil

Flour

Ginger

Red Pepper Flakes

Apple Juice

Brown Sugar

Cider Vinegar

Soy Sauce

Cornstarch

Weekly Shopping List

Garlic

One Pot Chicken & Veggies

Ingredients: *Serves 4-6*

2 tablespoons olive oil

1 pound chicken breast, cut into 1" chunks

2 cloves garlic, minced

1/2 cup onion, diced

1 red bell pepper, chopped

1 cup tomatoes, chopped

1 cup fresh broccoli florets, chopped

1/4 teaspoon red pepper flakes

2 cups heavy cream

1 cup parmesan cheese

16 oz. penne pasta

Directions:

1. In a skillet, heat oil. Add chicken breast, garlic, onion and bell pepper. Cook on medium heat until chicken is no longer pink.
2. Add tomatoes, broccoli and red pepper flakes along with heavy cream. Cook on low heat for 5-7 minutes or until broccoli is softened. Stir frequently.
3. Add parmesan cheese. Cook and stir until thickened.
4. Meanwhile, cook pasta according to package directions, drain.
5. Pour chicken mixture over pasta and serve.

Monthly Shopping List	Weekly Shopping List
Olive Oil	Garlic
Chicken Breast	Onion
Red Pepper Flakes	Red Bell Pepper
Penne Pasta	Tomato
	Broccoli
	Heavy Cream
	Parmesan Cheese

Simplified Chicken Cordon Bleu

Ingredients: *Serves 6-8*

> 1 egg
> 1 1/2 cups milk, divided
> 2 pounds boneless, skinless chicken breast, cut into 2" chunks
> 2 cups dry breadcrumbs
> 2-3 tablespoons olive oil
> 1 cup diced ham
> 8 oz. swiss cheese, cubed
> 1 (10 3/4 oz.) can cream of chicken soup (alternative page 133)

Directions:

1. Whisk egg with 1/2 cup milk.
2. Dip chicken into egg mixture, then into breadcrumbs.
3. In a skillet, heat olive oil. Cook chicken until lightly brown on both sides.
4. Add chicken to 13x9" baking dish. Top with diced ham and cheese.
5. Whisk together soup with 1 cup milk until thoroughly combined. Pour over top.
6. Bake uncovered at 350°F for 25-30 minutes.

Monthly Shopping List
Chicken Breast
Olive Oil
Diced Ham (if freezing)
Cream of Chicken Soup

Weekly Shopping List
Egg
Milk
Breadcrumbs
Swiss Cheese

Easy Kung Pao Chicken

Ingredients: *Serves 4-6*

1 pound boneless skinless chicken breast, cut into 1" pieces
1 tablespoon corn starch
2 teaspoons vegetable oil
2 cloves garlic, minced
1/4 cup rice wine vinegar
1/4 cup soy sauce
1 tablespoon sugar
1/2 teaspoon powdered ginger
1/2 teaspoon crushed red pepper flakes – more if you like it hot!
1-2 green onions, chopped
1/4 cup dry roasted peanuts, coarsely chopped

Directions:

1. In a bowl, mix together chicken breast and corn starch. Coat all sides of chicken.
2. In a skillet or wok, heat oil. Add chicken and garlic, and stir-fry 4-6 minutes or until juices run clear.
3. In a bowl, mix together vinegar, soy sauce, sugar, ginger, red pepper flakes and green onion. Add to skillet and cook on low until heated through.
4. Remove from heat and stir in nuts.
5. Serve as is or over a bed of rice.

Monthly Shopping List		Weekly Shopping List
Chicken Breast	Sugar	Garlic
Cornstarch	Powdered Ginger	Green Onion
Vegetable Oil	Crushed Red Pepper Flakes	
Rice Wine Vinegar	Dry Roasted Peanuts	
Soy Sauce		

Chapter 6

Pork

In this chapter we'll discuss the different cuts of pork, along with pork labeling, cooking methods and dinner prep recipes.

Pork Basics

Just like beef, pork is divided into primal cuts, with the most tender coming from the center of the animal: the loin and the rib.

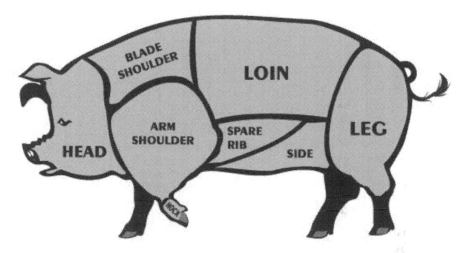

Blade Shoulder

Located in the upper shoulder and part of the neck, it is moderately tough due to the abundant connective tissue. Good for braising, stewing or grinding into sausage. The blade roast comes from the area nearest to the loin. It is well marbled and becomes tender and flavorful with slow heat methods of cooking. It is great for making pulled pork (see page 80).

Arm Shoulder

This area contains inexpensive cuts that are very flavorful when slow cooked. You can usually request them fresh or smoked from your butcher.

Loin

The loin contains little connective tissue, so it's very tender. Cuts can be grilled, sautéed or braised.

Leg

The leg is filled with connective tissue, so it's great for slow methods. Incidentally, this is where the ham comes from.

Side

The side contains the pork belly, bacon and spareribs. Spareribs are tender, so they can be barbecued or roasted. Often they are flavored with barbecue sauce or a dry rub before cooking.

Pork Labeling

Hormone Free

Hormones are not permitted in pork by federal regulations, so all pork is hormone free. This label does not indicate extra quality measures.

Natural

The label of "natural" when meat does not contain nitrates or nitrites as curing agents. It also cannot contain any artificial flavors, colors, preservatives or any other artificial ingredient.

Free Range

In order to use this label, the USDA requires that hogs have had access to pasture at least 80% of their life span.

Organic

This label requires compliance with USDA organic standards. Look for "100% organic" vs. "organic". The latter means that at least 95% of ingredients are organically produced.

Dinner Prep: Pork

In the following pages you'll find ideas for prepping ham, bacon, sausage and pulled pork. Remember, fresh pork can be stored in the refrigerator for 3-5 days or in the freezer for 4-6 months. Cooked pork can stay in the refrigerator for 3-4 days or in the freezer for 2-3 months.

Pork Chop Basics

Pork chops come from the loin, which is the strip that runs from the hip to the shoulder. Name distinctions such as Rib Chops, Loin Chops or Blade Chops indicate where on this strip they are cut from.

To make a basic pan-fried pork chop, heat oil in a skillet. Season pork chops with your favorite pork seasoning and place in hot pan. Cook on one side for 5-6 minutes or until brown crust forms. Flip and repeat. Make sure the chops are thoroughly cooked with a minimum internal temperature of 145°F. Allow to rest before serving.

Ribs

Fresh pork ribs can be stored in the refrigerator for 3-5 days or the freezer for 2-3 months. Cooking methods and seasoning preferences vary greatly. Personally, we love to use the barbecue sauce on page 114 with baby back ribs. Place in a covered baking dish in a 375°F oven for one hour, turning occasionally. Internal temperature should reach 145°F, and ribs should be allowed to rest for a few minutes before serving.

Ham

According to safety standards, cooked ham can be stored in the freezer for 1-2 months. I recommend storing it in one cup portions so it is divided up for recipes. You can use it to make a delicious egg scramble or omelet, or throw it in the Slow Cooker Mac & Cheese recipe every now and then.

Bacon

A delicious breakfast side or salad topping, bacon can come in handy for adding a little zing to a variety of dishes. It's also an easy item to make ahead and freeze.

Directions:

    1) Lay bacon in a single layer on a foil lined baking sheet.

    2) Bake at 350°F for 20-25 minutes.

    3) Lay bacon on paper towels to absorb grease and cool.

    Store in serving size freezer containers for up to 3 months.

If you prefer, you can decrease the baking time by 5 minutes or so to get it partially cooked for the freezer, and then finish it off in the microwave when you intend to use it.

Sausage

You can store fresh uncooked sausage in the freezer for 1-2 months. Place frozen sausage in the refrigerator to thaw and it will be ready to go for the next day's dinner.

Pork 10 Ways:

1. **Pulled Pork** – Page 80.
2. **Ham Carbonara** – Page 82.
3. **Cheesy Ham & Potato Soup** – Page 83.
4. **Cheesy Ham & Rice Casserole** – Page 84.
5. **Creamy Sausage & Pasta** – Page 85.
6. **Slow Cooker Pasta Fagioli** – Page 129.
7. **Sausage & Spaghetti Casserole** – Page 86.
8. **Sausage Breakfast Casserole** –Page 87.
9. **Macaroni & Cheese with Ham** – Page 123.
10. **Simplified Chicken Cordon Bleu** – Page 73.

Your Favorite Pork Recipes

_____

_____

_____

_____

_____

_____

_____

_____

_____

Pulled Pork

Start with a winning pulled pork recipe and the world is yours for the taking. You can whip up tasty sandwiches, wraps and pizzas, along with several other easy meals with the leftovers from this recipe.

Ingredients:

> 5-7 pound whole boston butt (bone-in) or blade roast

Dry Rub
> 1 tablespoon ground cumin
> 1 tablespoon garlic powder
> 1 tablespoon onion powder
> 1 tablespoon chili powder
> 1 tablespoon cayenne pepper
> 1 tablespoon salt
> 1 tablespoon ground pepper
> 1 tablespoon paprika
> 1/2 cup brown sugar

Brine Solution
> 2 quarts cold water
> 1/2 cup salt
> 1/2 cup brown sugar
> 3 tablespoons dry rub mix
> 2 bay leaves

Directions:

1. In a bowl, mix together cumin, garlic powder, onion powder, chili powder, cayenne pepper, salt, pepper, paprika and brown sugar to make the dry rub. Set aside.
2. In a large pitcher, mix salt into cold water until dissolved to make the brine. Then add brown sugar, 3 tbs. dry rub and bay leaves. Stir well.
3. Place roast in a large container or storage bag. Pour in brine solution until completely covered.

4. Store in the refrigerator for at least 8 hours.
5. Remove pork shoulder from brine and pat dry.
6. Place in a large baking pan with fat side up.
7. Generously sprinkle dry rub and massage in well on all sides.
8. Bake uncovered at 220°F on middle rack for 8-10 hours or until very tender. If you have a large slow cooker, you can cook on low for 8-10 hours instead. Either way, make sure shoulder reaches an internal temp of 200°F.
9. Remove from heat, cover and allow to cool for 20-30 minutes.
10. Shred pork with two forks.
11. Serve immediately or store in meal size freezer containers for up to 3 months.

Ham Carbonara

Ingredients: *Serves 4-6*

    1 pound box angel hair pasta

    1/3 cup olive oil

    1 medium onion, diced

    1 cup cooked diced ham

    1/4 cup butter

    1/2 cup chicken stock (homemade page 113)

    3 egg yolks, beaten

    1/2 cup parmesan cheese

    1/3 cup fresh parsley, minced

Directions:

1. Cook pasta according to package directions. Drain.
2. In a skillet, cook onions in olive oil.
3. Add ham and butter to skillet. Cook on medium for 2-3 minutes.
4. In a bowl, mix together chicken stock and egg yolks. Add to skillet and cook until heated through.
5. Combine skillet ingredients with cooked pasta.
6. Toss in parmesan and parsley. Serve.

Monthly Shopping List
Angel Hair Pasta
Olive Oil
Ham (if freezing)
Chicken Stock

Weekly Shopping List
Onion
Butter
Egg
Parmesan Cheese
Fresh Parsley

Cheesy Ham & Potato Soup

Ingredients: *Serves 4-6*

4 large potatoes, peeled and diced (about 3 cups)
1/2 cup onion, diced
1/4 cup celery, diced
2 cups cooked diced ham
3 1/2 cups chicken stock (homemade page 113)
salt and pepper to taste
1/4 cup flour
2 cups milk
2 cups sharp cheddar cheese, grated

Directions:

1. In a pot, add potatoes, onion, celery, ham and chicken stock.
2. Cook on medium until potatoes are tender.
3. In a saucepan, melt butter. Slowly add flour, stirring constantly until thickened.
4. Slowly pour milk into flour mixture, stirring constantly. Cook on medium for 4-5 minutes until thickened.
5. Add grated cheese and continue to cook and stir until thoroughly combined.
6. Pour cheese mixture into ham and potato mixture. Stir to combine. Serve.

Monthly Shopping List
Ham (if freezing)
Chicken Stock
Salt & Pepper
Flour

Weekly Shopping List
Potatoes
Onion
Celery
Milk
Sharp Cheddar Cheese

Cheesy Ham & Rice Casserole

Ingredients: *Serves 6-8*

 2 cup cooked rice

 2 cup cooked diced ham

 1 (16-oz.) bag frozen broccoli

 1 medium onion, chopped

 1 cup milk

 1 can cream of mushroom soup (alternative page 133)

 2 cup shredded cheddar cheese

Directions:

1. In a greased 13x9" baking dish, combine rice, ham, broccoli and onion.
2. In a separate bowl, mix together milk and cream of mushroom soup along with cheese. Pour over top of ham mixture.
3. Bake uncovered at 350°F for 25-30 minutes.

Monthly Shopping List
Rice
Ham (if freezing)
Frozen Broccoli
Cream of Mushroom Soup

Weekly Shopping List
Milk
Onion
Cheddar Cheese

Creamy Sausage & Pasta

Ingredients: *Serves 4-6*

1 tablespoon olive oil
1 pound spicy italian sausage
1 medium onion, diced
2 cloves garlic, minced
1 (14.5-oz) can diced tomatoes, drained
1 cup heavy cream
8 oz. farfalle pasta (bowtie)
parmesan cheese

Directions:

1. In a skillet, heat olive oil.
2. Add sausage, cook and crumble until no longer pink.
3. Add onion and garlic and continue to cook another 2-3 minutes.
4. Add diced tomatoes and heavy cream.
5. Simmer mixture until thickened.
6. Meanwhile, cook pasta according to package instructions. Drain.
7. Transfer pasta to a platter and pour sausage mixture over top. Sprinkle with parmesan cheese to your liking.

Monthly Shopping List
Olive Oil
Italian Sausage (if freezing)
Diced Tomatoes
Farfalle Pasta

Weekly Shopping List
Onion
Garlic
Heavy Cream
Parmesan Cheese

Sausage & Spaghetti Casserole

Ingredients: *Serves 6-8*

12 oz. spaghetti noodles

2 tablespoons olive oil

1 lb. ground sausage

16 oz. pasta sauce (homemade page 142)

1 cup mushrooms, sliced

2 cups shredded mozzarella cheese

1/2 cup parmesan cheese

Directions:

1. Cook pasta according to package instructions. Drain.
2. Meanwhile in a skillet, heat olive oil. Add sausage. Cook and crumble until no longer pink. Drain.
3. Add pasta sauce and mushrooms. Cook on medium for 3-5 minutes.
4. In a greased 13"x9" pan, layer 1/2 of the cooked spaghetti, followed by a layer of 1/2 sausage mixture, then a layer of cheese. Repeat, finishing with a layer of cheese.
5. Bake in a preheated 350°F oven for 30-40 minutes or until cheese is lightly brown.

Monthly Shopping List
Spaghetti Noodles
Olive Oil
Ground Sausage (if freezing)
Pasta Sauce

Weekly Shopping List
Mushrooms
Mozzarella Cheese
Parmesan Cheese

Sausage Breakfast Casserole

Don't let the simplicity of this recipe fool you. It is surprisingly delicious!

Ingredients: *Serves 6-8*

2 tablespoons olive oil

1 lb. ground sausage

4 cups frozen hash browns

1/2 cup chopped green bell pepper

1/2 cup chopped onion

12 fresh eggs

1 cup shredded cheddar cheese

Directions:

1. In a skillet heat oil.
2. Add sausage and cook until no longer pink. Drain.
3. Add hash browns to a greased 13x9" pan. Press into bottom to form crust.
4. Top with sausage, green pepper and onion.
5. In a bowl, whisk eggs. Pour over hash browns.
6. Top with cheese.
7. Bake at 350°F for 30 minutes.

Monthly Shopping List
Olive Oil
Ground Sausage (if freezing)
Frozen Hash Browns

Weekly Shopping List
Green Bell Pepper
Onion
Eggs
Shredded Cheddar Cheese

Chapter 7

Special Diets & Healthy Options

When I first began cooking as a young adult, my recipes were often delicious casseroles and high calorie dishes with a good dose of gooey cheese or sour cream, or both. I survived that way for a while, convincing myself that because I was young and thin, I was also healthy. It wasn't until I became pregnant with my first child that I transitioned into a healthier lifestyle and a more balanced diet. Then when child number five came along with a diagnosis of autism, I was suddenly thrust into a world of gluten-free, dairy-free, soy-free and about seven other kinds of "free". It was a foreign world to me, miles away from my careless gooey casserole days. But I had to learn fast.

Special Dietary Considerations
Even with all the new dietary restrictions, I was determined to provide flavorful meals and tasty treats so my child would not have the added displeasure of eating cardboard-ish food on top of everything else he was dealing with. But I still needed to maintain some measure of efficiency in the kitchen. So I got to work finding tricks for prepping and freezing recipes with modified ingredients. Through a bit of trial-and-error, I managed to accumulate a collection of recipes that fit his needs.

If someone in your family is living with a food allergy or dietary restriction, you know the effort of producing nutritionally sound meals is compounded. If this person is a child, you have the added consideration of providing food for special occasions, birthday parties and school lunches. With all of these responsibilities, it makes sense to have a plan in place to prep food ahead.

Since there are so many different dietary restrictions, there is not a one-size-fits-all answer for planning and prepping. But there are a few basic steps you can use to find and modify recipes to fit your own unique needs. If you have not already done so, begin by speaking with a nutritionist who will give you the foundation for meeting nutritional requirements within the framework of your diet.

Step 1: Find Your Staples

For any special diet, there are a few basic staple items you will use for making a variety of dishes. Once you have identified them, you can set about finding ways to prep them ahead. As an example, my son has a very self-limited diet in addition to his food sensitivities, so we work within these narrow preferences to come up with modified versions of his favorites. Once we found some basic gluten-free flour combinations, we could use them to make a variety of breads, pizza crust, cookies, cakes, waffles and muffins. I have a special section in my meal planning binder for storing these foundational recipes, and for planning and prepping.

Step 2: Be Creative

Meeting the daily nutritional requirements for my child requires another level of creativity. He doesn't eat plain vegetables, but he will eat them if they are hidden in other foods. So it was necessary to spend some time testing recipes that would be pleasing to his picky palate, and would also serve as a vessel for hiding the veggies. After some effort, we ended up with a collection of muffins, breads and even meatballs that do the trick. We make them in bulk to save time, then freeze them to use throughout the month.

Your situation may not require you to hide vegetables in meatballs, but the moral of the story is: where there's a will, there's a way. Don't be afraid to experiment and explore. You may not hit a homerun with every attempt, but over time you will end up with a workable and delicious collection of meals that fit your needs.

Step 3: Find Substitutions

In some instances, you can use simple substitution to create your favorite dishes without affecting quality or flavor. In order to determine whether this is possible, you will need to consider the role of the ingredient you are trying to replace in your recipe. For example, applesauce can be a good substitute for oil or eggs, but it will sometimes change the consistency and sweetness of the finished product. The best bet is to educate yourself on the role your allergen plays in the recipe, and then find a way to accomplish that goal with a similar ingredient. Here is a list of common substitutions for cooking and baking.

Milk: soy milk, rice milk, almond milk, hemp milk.

Buttermilk: 1 tablespoon white vinegar or lemon juice to one cup soy milk will replace 1 cup buttermilk.

Butter: organic shortening, ghee

Cream: coconut milk, soy coffee cream

Flour: rice flour, garbanzo flour, potato starch flour, sorghum flour, tapioca flour.

Pasta: rice pasta, bean pasta, corn pasta

Eggs: in baking, substitute 1/2 medium banana or 1/4 cup applesauce for every egg. This works best in recipes calling for less than three eggs.

Peanut Butter: sunflower seed butter or soy nut butter.

Cheese: soy or rice based cheese substitutes.

Sugar: stevia, honey, agave nectar, turbinado sugar

Prepping Ahead With Allergies

Here are some foods that can be modified to fit special dietary needs, but will generally freeze well.

- Breads
- Muffins
- Pancakes
- Waffles
- Pizza Crust or Flatbread
- Cookies
- Meatballs
- Chicken Nuggets
- Fruits & Vegetables
- Ice Cream
- Soups
- Pasta Sauce
- Pizza Sauce
- Salsa
- Jam

Meatless Meals

Eliminating meat from your menu once every week can reduce your risk for chronic preventable diseases, such as cancer and diabetes. If you've never gone meatless, you may be surprised to find the myriad of delicious dinner options available. Begin by finding a few recipes that appeal to you, and slowly work them into the meal plan. When you find a winner, store it in your meal planning binder. In time, you'll establish a collection of healthy meatless options your family will be happy with.

Meatless 10 Ways:

1) **Veggie Enchiladas** – Page 94.
2) **Quesadillas** – Page 68. Modify with fillings of spinach, mushrooms, onion and pepper jack cheese for a refreshing meatless option.
3) **Hearty Tex-Mex Soup** – Page 118. Remove the ground beef and add one extra can beans of your choice.
4) **Eggplant Parmesan** – Page 95.
5) **Italian Mushroom Soup** – Page 117. Use 2 cups cremini mushrooms in place of meatballs, and substitute vegetable broth for chicken stock.
6) **Meatless Chili** – Page 119. Omit the ground beef in favor of an extra can of kidney beans.
7) **Slow Cooker Spicy Noodle Soup** – Page 127. Get rid of the chicken and add 6 oz. uncooked whole wheat macaroni noodles during the last hour of cooking. You can use vegetable broth in place of chicken stock.
8) **Meatless Pasta Fagioli** – Page 129. Replace the sausage with 2 cups cremini mushrooms. Then replace the chicken stock with vegetable broth.
9) **Open Face Grilled Vegetable Sandwich** –Page 96.
10) **Veggie Pizza or Flatbread** – Use fresh sliced tomatoes in lieu of pizza sauce, then top with artichoke hearts, asparagus and mushrooms. Top with fresh mozzarella cheese and bake as usual.

Ten Tips for Improving Nutrition

Quick and simple meals needn't be unhealthy. You can benefit from prepping, while making health a priority with these simple steps.

1) Be sure portion sizes are appropriate. Most people will eat more when portions are larger.

2) Make sure half of your dinner plate consists of fruits and vegetables.

3) Refined grains are lacking in nutritional benefits. Choose whole grains whenever possible.

4) Most people in the US do not get enough calcium. Serving milk or other calcium-fortified beverages with dinner is an easy way to improve health.

5) Got a picky eater? Get them involved in the process of shopping and cooking food. Including them is a great way to get more cooperation.

6) Substitute lean proteins for red meat. You can use ground turkey or bison in place of beef in many recipes.

7) Use homemade versions of store-bought favorites. Making your own beef/chicken stock, baking mixes and seasoning mixes will eliminate unnecessary sodium and preservatives. They're easy to make, and they taste ten times better!

8) Eliminate sweetened beverages.

9) Go meatless one day per week. Lowering your red and processed meat consumption reduces risk for diabetes, heart disease, cancer and a myriad of other health conditions.

10) Make vegetables more appealing. Experiment with different combinations and seasonings until you find the ones that work for your family. In my home, I've been known to give broccoli a superhero name, or make smiley faces out of peas. Whatever it takes.

Veggie Enchiladas

Ingredients: *serves 4-6*

    3 tablespoons olive oil,divided
    1 tablespoon cumin
    1 tablespoon chili powder
    1 teaspoon cocoa powder
    1/4 cup all purpose flour
    1/4 cup tomato paste
    15 oz. vegetable broth
    1 onion, diced
    1 red bell pepper, diced
    2 (15-oz.) cans black beans, rinsed and drained
    1 (10-oz.) box frozen corn, thawed and drained
    3 cups grated pepper jack cheese, divided
    16 corn tortillas (6 inch)

Directions:

1) In a skillet, heat 2 tablespoons olive oil on medium heat.
2) Add cumin, chili powder, cocoa powder, flour and tomato paste. Cook, stirring constantly for 1 minute.
3) Stir in broth and 3/4 cup water. Bring to a boil.
4) Reduce heat and simmer until thickened, about 5-8 minutes. Remove from heat and set aside.
5) In a separate skillet, heat 1 tablespoon olive oil on medium heat.
6) Add onions and peppers. Cook until tender. Remove from heat.
7) Add black beans, corn and 2 cups cheese to onion mixture for the filling.
8) In a 9" x 13" pan, pour 1/2 enchilada sauce.
9) Add 1/3 cup filling mixture to the center of each corn tortilla. Roll up and place in pan.
10) Pour remaining enchilada sauce and sprinkle with cheese.
11) Bake in a preheated 400°F oven for 15-20 minutes. Serve.

Eggplant Parmesan

Ingredients: *serves 4-6*

> 1 large eggplant (2 lbs.)
> 1 tablespoon olive oil
> salt and pepper
> 1 cup milk
> 3 tablespoons all-purpose flour
> 2 cloves garlic, minced
> 1 cup pasta sauce, divided (homemade page 142)
> 1/2 cup grated mozzarella cheese
> 1/2 cup grated parmesan cheese

Directions:

1) Slice eggplant into 1/2 "slices lengthwise.
2) Brush eggplant on both sides with olive oil, and sprinkle with salt and pepper.
3) Arrange on a baking sheet and bake at 450°F for 20-25 minutes or until tender and golden brown, turning once halfway through bake time.
4) Meanwhile, in a saucepan with heat off, stir together 1/4 cup milk, flour and garlic.
5) Gradually mix in remaining milk, along with 1/2 cup pasta sauce. Cook on medium heat until thickened, around 2-3 minutes.
6) In a 13" x 9" baking dish, pour 1/4 cup pasta sauce. Top with a layer of eggplant, then a layer of cream sauce. Continue alternating layers of eggplant, then cream sauce.
7) Top with remaining pasta sauce and grated cheeses.
8) Bake at 450°F for 10-15 minutes. Serve.

Monthly Shopping List	Weekly Shopping List
Olive Oil	Eggplant
Salt & Pepper	Milk
All Purpose Flour	Garlic
Pasta Sauce	Mozzarella Cheese
	Parmesan Cheese

Open Faced Grilled Vegetable Sandwich

Ingredients: *serves 4-6*

2 tablespoons olive oil
1 tablespoon balsamic vinegar
1 red bell pepper, quartered
1 yellow bell pepper, quartered
4 portabella mushrooms, stems removed
1 medium eggplant, sliced 1/4" lengthwise
salt and pepper
3-4 oz. goat cheese
4-6 slices italian bread

Directions:

1) Combine olive oil and balsamic vinegar. Brush on vegetables.
2) Grill vegetables for 3-4 minutes per side, or until tender.
3) Lightly toast bread. Spread a small amount of goat cheese on each slice.
4) Top with grilled vegetables. Serve.

Monthly Shopping List	Weekly Shopping List	
Olive Oil	Red Bell Pepper	Eggplant
Balsamic Vinegar	Yellow Bell Pepper	Goat Cheese
Salt & Pepper	Portabella Mushrooms	Italian Bread

Vegetable Broth

The secret to a good vegetable stock is using finely chopped vegetables. It increases the amount of surface area in contact with the water, making it easier for the flavors to be infused into the broth.

Ingredients:

2 tablespoons olive oil
3 cups chopped onions
3 cups carrots, chopped
2 cups celery, chopped
3 cloves garlic, smashed
2 tablespoons tomato paste
1 tablespoon black peppercorns
2 cups button mushrooms, sliced

Directions:

1) In a large stockpot, heat olive oil over medium heat.
2) Add onions, carrots and celery. Cook over medium heat until onions are lightly brown, about 7-9 minutes.
3) Stir in garlic and tomato paste. Cook over medium heat for 2-3 minutes.
4) Add peppercorns, mushrooms and 4 quarts water. Simmer for 1 1/2 hours.
5) Pour through a sieve to strain.
6) Refrigerate for up to one week, or freeze for up to 6 months.

Monthly Shopping List	Weekly Shopping List	
Olive Oil	Onion	Garlic
Tomato Paste	Carrots	Button Mushrooms
Black Peppercorns	Celery	

Chapter 8

Fruits & Vegetables

Keep a bounty of ingredients for sides, desserts, snacks and smoothies available in your freezer and save loads of time during the dinner hour. In this chapter, we'll cover the tricks to successfully prepping fruits and vegetables. Once you learn them, you'll be able to load up when produce is in-season and at the lowest prices and reap the savings for months.

Fruit & Vegetable Basics

- Always use fruits and vegetables that are at their peak of flavor and free from browning, bruising or other damage.
- When possible, freeze vegetables within a few hours of harvesting.
- Wash in cold water, but do not soak. Soaking can cause nutrients to leach out.
- Allow to dry thoroughly before freezing.
- Label your freezer safe container with date and description.

Finding the Best Prices on Fruits and Vegetables

1. Search the web to find locations and business hours for your local farmers market. They often have the best prices for in-season produce.
2. Keep an eye on your local grocery store sale flyers. If they're offering a rock bottom price, contact the produce manager and request a large order. You can also utilize the price matching policy of many of the national grocery stores to get the same deal.
3. Grow your own produce! There is a wealth of information on the web and in the bookstores about how to have a large bounty of homegrown vegetables in a small back yard. You'll not only save money, you'll be teaching your children and grandchildren to be more self sufficient.

4. Pick it yourself. Once again, a simple web search should give you the names and locations of local u-pick farms. Make it a fun family activity! Just be sure to compare farm prices to local store sale prices. Over the past few years we have seen an increase in u-pick prices to the point of exceeding store sale prices in some instances.

TIP: *You can use a bundt pan to speed up the process of cutting kernels from the cob. Place the pointed end of the cob in the middle of the pan, then slice kernels with a sharp knife. They will fall off nicely into the surrounding pan.*

Dinner Prep: Vegetables

Different vegetables require different freezer preparation. In this section you will learn the proper techniques for some of the most popular vegetables.

Green Beans
Choose fresh and brightly colored green beans that are free from blemishes. Wash well, then cut off the stem and cut them into 2" pieces. Bring to boil one gallon water for every pound of green beans. Add them to the water and allow to cook, boiling for 4 minutes. Cool the beans quickly by plunging them into ice water to stop the cooking process. Drain and allow to dry completely, then store in the freezer for up to 10 months.

Peas
Edible pod peas are the easiest to freeze (Snow Peas, Sugar, Chinese or Sugar Snap Peas). Find the freshest, blemish-free pods. Wash and remove stems, blossom pods and strings. Blanch for 1 ½ minutes for small pods or 2 minutes for large pods. Use one gallon of water per two cups peas. Drain, cool and dry. Freezes for up to 10 months.

Tomatoes
Yes, you can freeze tomatoes. In fact, it works very well for removing the skins when you need to make sauces. Just wash your fresh and blemish-free tomatoes and cut away the stem scar. Dry thoroughly and freeze for up to two months. When thawed, the skins will slip off with ease when rinsed under water. Use them to make homemade pasta sauce from page 142 or pizza sauce from page 143.

Zucchini
If you like to use zucchini in cooking and baking, you can freeze it and use it for months. Cut it into the size you will be using when thawed. Blanch for 3 minutes. Drain, dry and freeze for up to 10 months. You can even grate it and freeze it to make breads and muffins later on.

Onions, Green Peppers

Chopping onions and green peppers in advance will make for some super easy omelets or other dishes. Both of these will last for up to 6 months in the freezer, but I've found that the flavor diminishes after about a month. Be sure to keep them in separate containers to preserve flavor. It helps to have some diced ham in the freezer to round out your breakfast prep while you're at it. See page 86 for details.

Broccoli & Cauliflower

When freezing broccoli and cauliflower it is essential to choose fresh and crisp vegetables. Wash well and split the heads so the florets are about 1 ½ inches across. If necessary, soak in brine for 30 minutes to remove insects (1 teaspoon salt to 1 gallon tap water). Then rinse well. Blanch for 3 minutes, then drain and dry. Store in freezer safe containers for up to 10 months.

Corn

Remove the husks and blanch for 4 minutes. Cool. Cut kernels from the cob and freeze in appropriate container for up to 8 months.

Carrots

Remove tops, peel and wash. Dice and slice according to how you will be using them in recipes. If you like, you can leave small carrots whole. Blanch for 5 minutes if whole, or 2-3 minutes for smaller pieces, depending on size.

Vegetable Combinations

Once vegetables are frozen, you can make your own combinations and freeze them together in meal size portions.

- Stir Fry Blend – 1/3 snap peas, 1/3 carrots and 1/3 broccoli
- California Blend – 1/3 broccoli, 1/3 cauliflower, 1/3 carrots
- Mixed Blend – 1/4 peas, 1/4 corn, 1/4 sliced carrots, 1/4 green beans

Dinner Prep: Fruits

Frozen fruit can be used in most baking recipes. You can also use it to make delicious and healthy smoothies.

What Fruit Can I Freeze?
Anything you find in the freezer section of your grocery store is fair game. Think cherries, berries, bananas, pineapple, pears, mango and papaya.

How to Freeze Fresh Fruit
1. Wash and dry fruit.
2. Remove any peels, stems and cores.
3. Cut larger fruit into chunks, such as bananas, pineapple, pears, mango and papaya. Berries can remain intact.
4. Flash freeze
5. Transfer to a freezer safe container and store in the freezer for 6-12 months.

Here are some great uses for frozen fruit.

Bananas
Peel and cut into 2-4 pieces, then freeze for up to 1 month.

- Make banana bread or muffins by thawing and using as per recipe.
- Frozen bananas make a great starter for morning smoothies.
- Dip in melted dark chocolate and roll in chopped peanuts. Freeze and enjoy.

Strawberries, Raspberries, Blackberries, Blueberries
Wash, dry and de-stem (when needed). Then flash freeze. Store in freezer for up to 4 months

- Smoothies or frozen beverages
- Pies
- Sundae topping

- Homemade ice cream
- Add to hot cereal or pancake batter
- Add to yogurt or cottage cheese
- Make homemade cakes, muffins or breads

Grapes

Remove from vine, wash and allow to dry. Flash freeze and store in freezer for up to 1 month. These make great healthy alternative to ice cream when eaten frozen. Kids love 'em!

Cherries

Remove the pit and flash freeze. Then store in an airtight freezer container for up to 12 months.

- Smoothies and frozen vegetables
- Make your own freezer friendly cherry pie filling. Recipe on page 105.
- Sundae topping. The cherry pie filling recipe is perfect for this too.
- Add to yogurt or hot cereal.
- Make homemade cakes, muffins or breads
- Cherry turnovers
- Cherry cobbler

Apples

Apples can be dry frozen or packed in syrup. But for my money, I prefer to make them into pie filling or applesauce first. You can use the Slow Cooker Applesauce recipe on page 115 and throw your leftovers into a freezer friendly container where they will keep for up to 12 months.

Freezer Friendly Cherry Pie Filling

Crank out some extra batches of this delicious pie filling and freeze it for future use. It's even great over ice cream or french toast.

Ingredients:

> 4 cups tart red cherries, pitted
> 1 cup granulated sugar
> 1/4 cup cornstarch
> 1 tablespoon lemon juice

Directions:

1. Cook cherries in a covered saucepan over medium heat until juices are released, about 7-8 minutes. Stir frequently.
2. In a bowl, mix together sugar and corn starch then add to cherries and cook on low, stirring often.
3. Add lemon juice and continue to cook and stir until filling is thickened, about 3 minutes.
4. Use immediately or store in the refrigerator for 3-4 days, or in a freezer safe container for 10-12 months.
5. To use frozen filling, allow to thaw completely, then follow baking instructions for your favorite pie crust.

Freezer Friendly Apple Pie Filling

Ingredients:

15 cups apples peeled, cored and thinly sliced

2 1/2 tablespoons lemon juice

3 3/4 cups granulated sugar

1 cup cornstarch

2 teaspoons ground cinnamon

1 teaspoon salt

1/4 teaspoon ground nutmeg

9 cups water

Directions:

1. Peel, core and thinly slice apples. Toss in lemon juice and set aside.
2. Combine sugar, cornstarch, cinnamon, salt and nutmeg.
3. In a large pot, add water and sugar mixture. Bring to a boil.
4. Continue boiling for 2 minutes, stirring constantly
5. Add apples and reduce heat to a simmer. Cook covered for 6-8 minutes or until apples are tender.
6. Allow to cool completely.
7. Store in freezer friendly containers. Freeze for up to 12 months. Makes 4 pies.

Blueberry Syrup

Perfect for pouring over pancakes or sundaes, this syrup will ruin you for any store-bought variety.

Ingredients:

5 cups blueberries

1 cup water

1 cup granulated sugar

2 tablespoons lemon juice

Directions:

1. Place blueberries and water in a pot. Mash with a potato masher.
2. Bring to a boil. Reduce heat and simmer for 15 minutes, stirring occasionally.
3. Using a fine sieve, strain berries into a bowl.
4. In a pot, combine blueberry juice and sugar. Bring to a boil.
5. Reduce heat and simmer for 10 minutes or until slightly thickened.
6. Stir in lemon juice. Remove from heat and allow to cool.
7. Store in the refrigerator for up to 3 weeks or store in a freezer safe container and freeze for up to 6 months.

Fruit Crisp

Ingredients:

5 cups sliced, peeled, cored apples, pears, peaches or apricots

1/4 cup granulated sugar

1/2 cup regular rolled oats

1/2 cup light brown sugar

1/4 teaspoon ground cinnamon or nutmeg

1/4 cup butter

1/4 cup chopped nuts or coconut

Directions:

1. Add fruit to an ungreased 9"x13" baking dish. If you are using frozen fruit, allow to thaw but do not drain.
2. In a bowl combine oats, brown sugar, granulated sugar and cinnamon or nutmeg. Mix well.
3. Cut in butter to make coarse crumbs. Add nuts or coconut and sprinkle over fruit.
4. Bake at 375°F for 30-35 minutes. Serve and enjoy.

Cherry Crisp

Follow recipe above, increasing granulated sugar to 1/2 cup and combine with 1/4 cup all purpose flour. Toss 5 cups fresh or frozen pitted sweet cherries in the sugar-flour mixture and continue recipe as usual.

Frozen Fruit Smoothies

Frozen fruit is ideal for making smoothies. Here are the basic components.

Liquid

Depending on your preference for consistency and flavor, you'll need to experiment with adding liquids to your smoothie. Consider cow's milk, coconut milk, soy milk, yogurt or juice.

Fruit

Choose your fruit based on your flavor preferences as well as the nutritional benefits of each.

Other Options

Adding a little honey, stevia or sugar will please the folks who are partial to a sweeter version. You can also add supplements such as maca powder, protein powder or flaxseed meal for added health benefits.

Chapter 9

Slow Cooker

The slow cooker is an invaluable tool for easy dinner prep. Ther are many delicious main dish recipes in this chapter that give you a nice variety of dinner planning options. Everything from hearty soups and stews, to easy roasts and casseroles. On nights when you're not using it for meals, you can whip up some homemade beef or chicken stock, or a batch of barbecue sauce for future use. It will fill the house with a nice aroma all day long.

What Size Do I Need?
The slow cooker you will need depends upon your family size and the purpose you will be using it for.

1-2 Quart	Generally used for making dips and spreads or for 1-2 servings.
3-4 Quart	Works for a small family of 3-4.
5-6 Quart	Families of four or more. Use them for full roasts, chicken, turkey or ham, depending on their size.
7-8 Quart	If you have a large family or if you entertain often, this one will handle the extra capacity. Works well for larger roasts, chicken, turkey or ham.

It is generally recommended that slow cookers be filled no more than 3/4 full. This allows for proper cooking temperatures to be reached. Overfilling may result in temperatures that are lower than recommended for safe cooking. This should be a determining factor when choosing the proper slow cooker size.

Beef Stock

If you love soup, then this is a must-have staple for your freezer. It adds an amazing depth of flavor – oceans apart from its canned cousins!

Ingredients:

6-7 pounds meaty beef bones (ask your butcher)
2 onions, chopped
4 cloves garlic, smashed
6-8 whole black peppercorns
water (enough to cover the bones)

Directions:

1. Arrange the bones on an ungreased baking sheet.
2. Bake at 350°F for 30 minutes, turning to brown all sides.
3. Remove from oven and place in slow cooker along with all other ingredients. Cover with water.
4. Cover and cook on lowest heat for 4-6 hours.
5. As it cooks, remove any fat that floats to the top with a large spoon.
6. Remove from heat and strain to remove all bones, meat, etc.
7. Allow to cool.
8. Store in the refrigerator for up to 3 days or freeze for up to 6 months.
9. If you plan to freeze, remember to leave at least 1 inch headroom to allow for expansion.

Weekly Shopping List: All items except black peppercorns

Chicken Stock

If you're using the recipe on page 54 for making shredded chicken, take a few extra steps to create the most flavorful and delicious stock you'll ever taste.

Ingredients:

> All liquid, bones and remaining meat from shredded chicken
>   recipe on page 54
> 1 onion, chopped
> 2 carrots, chopped
> 2 ribs celery, chopped
> 4 cloves garlic, diced
> 6-8 whole black peppercorns

Directions:

1. Add all ingredients to slow cooker and cook on low for 4-5 hours.
2. Remove from heat and allow to cool.
3. Skim off fat.
4. Strain and freeze in meal size containers for up to 6 months or refrigerate for up to 3 days. When freezing, be sure to leave at least 1 inch headroom to allow for expansion.

Weekly Shopping List: All items except black peppercorns

Momma's Slow Cooker Barbecue Sauce

Ingredients:

18 oz. tomato paste

1 cup chicken stock (homemade page 113)

1/2 cup brown sugar

1/2 cup prepared yellow mustard

1/3 cup apple cider vinegar

3 cloves garlic, minced

1 tablespoon ground black pepper

1/2 teaspoon cayenne pepper

1 teaspoon salt

Directions:

1. Mix all ingredients well and pour into slow cooker.
2. Cook on low for 3-4 hours.
3. Use immediately or remove from heat and cool. Store in airtight container in the refrigerator for up to 2 weeks or freezer for up to 6 months. Leave at least one inch headroom to allow for expansion in the freezer.

Monthly Shopping List: All ingredients

Applesauce

Ingredients:

> 4 lbs tart apples
> 1/2 cup sugar
> 1 teaspoon cinnamon
> 1 tablespoon lemon juice
> 1 cup water

Directions:

1. Peel, core and slice apples into bite size chunks.
2. Sprinkle cinnamon and sugar over apples and mix well.
3. Place apple mixture in slow cooker. Pour water and lemon juice over top.
4. Cook on low for 6 hours or high for 3 hours, stirring occasionally.
5. Mash coarsely with potato masher.
6. Serve immediately or allow to cool and store in freezer containers for up to 12 months.

Modification: When using sweet apples, decrease the amount of sugar used. If you prefer smooth applesauce, allow to cool then run through a blender until smooth.

Monthly Shopping List
Sugar
Cinnamon

Weekly Shopping List
Apples
Lemon Juice

Freezer Friendly Slow Cooker Apple Butter

This is an easy way to preserve your apples. If a smoother consistency is desired, you can use a blender or food processor just after cooking and just before freezing.

Ingredients:

6 pounds apples
4 cups sugar
3 teaspoons ground cinnamon
1/4 teaspoon ground cloves
1/2 teaspoon salt

Directions:

1. Peel, core and chop apples.
2. Combine sugar, cinnamon, cloves and salt. Add to apples and mix well.
3. Pour into slow cooker. Cook on high for one hour.
4. Stir well and reduce to low.
5. Continue cooking for 9-11 hours or until thickened, stirring occasionally.
6. Remove cover and cook for another 60-90 minutes to allow some evaporation.
7. Use immediately or allow to cool and store in freezer safe containers. Freeze for 10-12 months.

Monthly Shopping List
Sugar
Cinnamon
Cloves
Salt

Weekly Shopping List
Apples

Italian Meatball Soup

Use the freezer-friendly meatball recipe from page 36 to whip this up in no time.

Ingredients: *Serves 6-8*

1 ½ pounds precooked meatballs, thawed (page 33)

6 cups chicken stock (homemade page 113)

1 small onion, diced

2 tablespoons tomato paste

1 (28-oz.) can diced tomatoes

2 teaspoons dried oregano

2 teaspoons dried basil

1 teaspoon garlic powder

1/2 teaspoon crushed red pepper flakes

8 oz. spiral pasta

mozzarella and parmesan cheese (optional)

Directions:

1. Combine all ingredients except pasta and cheese in a slow cooker. Cook on low for 4-6 hours or high for 2-4 hours.
2. Add pasta during the last hour of cooking.
3. Serve with a sprinkling of mozzarella and parmesan cheese on top if you are so inclined!

Monthly Shopping List

		Weekly Shopping List
Meatballs	Chicken Stock	Onion
Tomato Paste	Diced Tomatoes	Mozzarella Cheese
Oregano	Basil	Parmesan Cheese
Garlic Powder	Crushed Red Pepper Flakes	
Spiral Pasta		

Hearty Tex-Mex Soup

Great for using up precooked ground beef. Also delicious with shredded chicken.

Ingredients: *Serves 6-8*

1 pound ground beef, cooked and drained

1 medium onion, diced

1 (16-oz.) can pinto beans

1 (16-oz.) can kidney beans

1 (16-oz.) can diced tomatoes with green chilies

1 (16-oz.) can whole kernel corn

1 (14-oz.) can tomato sauce

1 cup water

1 pkg. taco seasoning mix (homemade page 135)

1 pkg. ranch dressing mix (homemade page 136)

Directions:

1. Drain and rinse beans and corn.
2. Combine all ingredients in a slow cooker.
3. Cook on low for 3-4 hours.
4. Optional: Serve with a garnish of shredded cheese, tortilla chips, green onions and sour cream.

Monthly Shopping List		Weekly Shopping List
Ground Beef	Pinto Beans	Onion
Kidney Beans	Diced Tomato/Green Chiles	
Can Whole Kernel Corn	Tomato Sauce	
Taco Seasoning Mix	Ranch Dressing Mix	

Slow Cooker Chili

Ingredients: *Serves 6-8*

1 pound ground beef
1 small onion, diced
1 28-oz.can diced tomatoes
1 15-oz.can tomato sauce
2 15-oz.cans kidney beans, rinsed and drained
2 teaspoons chili powder
1/2 teaspoon ground cumin
1/2 teaspoon ground coriander
1/2 teaspoon garlic powder
1/2 teaspoon oregano
pinch of cayenne pepper

Directions:

1. In a skillet, cook ground beef and drain.
2. Place one can of kidney beans in the food processor and process until smooth. Add to slow cooker. Mix well.
3. Add all remaining ingredients to slow cooker.
4. Cook on low for 6-8 hours or high for 3-4 hours.

Monthly Shopping List

		Weekly Shopping List
Ground Beef	Diced Tomatoes	Onion
Tomato Sauce	Kidney Beans	
Chili Powder	Ground Cumin	
Ground Coriander	Garlic Powder	
Oregano	Cayenne	

Beef Stew

Most butchers will offer precut stew meat. If yours does, simply remove from store packaging and freeze in a freezer safe container or bag. Otherwise you can purchase an inexpensive cut (such as chuck steak) and cut into 1"x1" pieces.

Ingredients: *Serves 6-8*

2-3 pounds stew meat
1 (14 oz.) can diced tomatoes
1 envelope onion soup mix (or 1/4 cup from page 131)
2 cups beef stock (homemade page 112)
2 cloves garlic, minced
4 medium potatoes, peeled and cubed
4 carrots, chopped
2 stalks celery, chopped
2 tablespoons cornstarch
1/4 cup water

Directions:

1. Add all ingredients except water and cornstarch to a slow cooker and cook on low for 7-9 hours or high for 3-5 hours.
2. In a bowl, whisk water and cornstarch together until no lumps.
3. Slowly add cornstarch mixture to slow cooker. Stir until thickened.

Monthly Shopping List
Stew Meat
Diced Tomatoes
Onion Soup Mix
Beef Stock
Cornstarch

Weekly Shopping List
Garlic
Potatoes
Carrots
Celery

Slow Cooker Beef Barley Soup

Ingredients: *Serves 4-6*

1 ½ pounds chuck roast or steak, cut into 1/2" cubes

1 medium onion, chopped

2 stalks celery, diced

2 carrots, diced

3/4 cup barley

6 cups beef stock (homemade page 112)

1/2 teaspoon garlic powder

Directions:

1. Combine all ingredients in a slow cooker.
2. Cook on low 6-8 hours or high for 3-4 hours.

Monthly Shopping List
Chuck Roast or Steak
Barley
Beef Stock
Garlic Powder

Weekly Shopping List
Onion
Celery
Carrots

Slow Cooker Beef Burgundy

Ingredients: *Serves 6-8*

2 pounds chuck roast or steak, cut into 1" cubes.

1/4 cup flour

1/2 teaspoon salt

1/2 teaspoon pepper

2 tablespoon olive oil

3 cloves garlic, minced

1/3 cup fresh parsley, minced

2 bay leaves

1 onion, chopped

1 cup sliced button mushrooms

1 cup burgundy wine

1/2 cup beef stock (homemade page 112)

Directions:

1. In a shallow bowl, combine flour, salt and pepper.
2. Dredge beef cubes in flour.
3. In a skillet, heat oil. Brown beef on all sides.
4. Place beef and remaining ingredients in a slow cooker and cook on low for 4-6 hours or high for 2-3 hours.
5. Remove bay leaves and serve.

Monthly Shopping List		Weekly Shopping List
Chuck Roast or Steak	Flour	Garlic
Salt	Pepper	Parsley
Olive Oil	Bay Leaves	Onion
Burgundy Wine	Beef Stock	Button Mushrooms

Slow Cooker Mac & Cheese

Ingredients: *Serves 6-8*

   12 oz. elbow macaroni

   12 oz. evaporated milk

   1 1/2 cups whole milk

   5 cups shredded cheddar cheese

   1 teaspoon salt

   dash of cayenne pepper

Directions:

1. Cook macaroni according to package directions and drain.
2. Spray the inside of slow cooker with nonstick cooking spray.
3. Add all ingredients, saving 1/2 cup cheese. Mix together well.
4. Top with 1/2 cup remaining cheese.
5. Cook on low for 2-4 hours.

Monthly Shopping List   **Weekly Shopping List**
Elbow Macaroni   Whole Milk
Evaporated Milk   Shredded Cheddar Cheese
Salt
Cayenne

Easy Slow Cooker Hamburger Soup

Ingredients: *Serves 6-8*

> 1 lb. ground beef, cooked and drained
>
> 1 (28-oz.) can diced tomatoes
>
> 1 (8-oz.) can tomato sauce
>
> 1 (16-oz.) can red kidney beans, drained
>
> 2 (10-oz.) cans beef stock (homemade page 112)
>
> 1 clove garlic, minced
>
> 2 carrots, diced
>
> 2 stalks celery, diced
>
> 1 small onion, chopped
>
> 1 tablespoon dried parsley
>
> 2 teaspoons oregano
>
> pinch of cayenne pepper (optional)
>
> 6 oz. elbow macaroni pasta
>
> parmesan cheese (optional)

Directions:

1. In a skillet, cook ground beef with diced onions. Add garlic during the last minute of cooking. Drain.
2. Add remaining ingredients except pasta to the slow cooker and cook on low 7-8 hours or high for 3-4 hours.
3. During the last 30 minutes of cooking, boil water and cook pasta according to package instructions. Add to soup just before serving. Sprinkle with parmesan cheese.

Monthly Shopping List		Weekly Shopping List
Ground Beef	Diced Tomatoes	Garlic
Tomato Sauce	Red Kidney Beans	Carrots
Beef Stock	Dried Parsley	Celery
Oregano	Cayenne Pepper	Onion
Elbow Macaroni Pasta		Parmesan Cheese

Slow Cooker Pot Roast

Ingredients: *Serves 6-8*

4 pounds chuck roast

1/4 cup prepared horseradish

1/4 cup whole grain mustard

2 (14-oz.) cans beef stock (homemade page 112)

1 medium onion, chopped

Directions:

1. In a bowl, mix horseradish and mustard.
2. Coat roast in horseradish mixture on all sides.
3. Add all ingredients to slow cooker and cook on low 7-9 hours.

Monthly Shopping List
Chuck Roast
Prepared Horseradish
Whole Grain Mustard
Beef Stock

Weekly Shopping List
Onion

Carne Guisada

Ingredients: *Serves 6-8*

3 pounds chuck roast
1/4 cup flour
2 tablespoons vegetable oil
2 cloves garlic, minced
1 medium onion, diced
2 jalapeno peppers, seeded and minced
3 cups beef stock (homemade page 112)
3 tablespoons tomato paste
1 tablespoon cumin
1 teaspoon chili powder
flour tortillas or cooked rice (optional)

Directions:

1. Cut roast into bite sized pieces and roll in flour.
2. Brown in vegetable oil.
3. Add roast and remaining ingredients to a slow cooker. Cook on low for 6-8 hours.
4. Serve in tortillas or on a bed of mexican rice.

Monthly Shopping List

Chuck Roast	Flour	
Vegetable Oil	Beef Stock	
Tomato Paste	Cumin	
Chili Powder		

Weekly Shopping List
Garlic
Onion
Jalapeno Peppers

Slow Cooker Spicy Chicken Stew

I love that this one comes together in the slow cooker. It has just the right kick to make it interesting.

Ingredients: *Serves 6-8*

> 3 cups cooked shredded chicken (page 54)
> 2 1/2 cups chicken stock (homemade page 113)
> 3 cups baking potatoes, peeled and chopped
> 1 (10 oz.) pkg. frozen sweet corn
> 1 cup celery, chopped
> 1 cup carrots, chopped
> 1 jalapeno pepper, seeded and diced
> 2 teaspoons ground cumin
> 1/4 teaspoon cayenne pepper
> 1 teaspoon chili powder
> 1 cup cheddar cheese, shredded

Directions:

1. Combine all ingredients except cheese in a slow cooker.
2. Cook on low 4-6 hours or high for 2-3 hours.
3. Ladle into bowls and top with cheddar cheese and your favorite toppings (tortilla chips, sour cream, avocado, etc.).

Monthly Shopping List
Chicken
Chicken Stock
Frozen Sweet Corn
Cumin
Cayenne
Chili Powder

Weekly Shopping List
Baking Potatoes
Celery
Carrots
Jalapeno Pepper
Cheddar Cheese

Shredded Chicken Tacos

The simplicity of this recipe makes the delicious end product all that more amazing. You can also use the chicken to make the best nachos, enchiladas, tostadas, burritos...you name it!

Ingredients: *Serves 6-8*

2 pounds cooked shredded chicken

1 (16-oz.) jar salsa

1 Envelope Taco Seasoning (or homemade page 135)

12 Flour Tortillas

Your Favorite Toppings

Directions:

1. Add all ingredients to your slow cooker and mix well.
2. Cook on low for 4-6 hours.
3. Layer tortillas with chicken and your favorite toppings.

Monthly Shopping List
Chicken
Jar Salsa
Taco Seasoning Mix

Weekly Shopping List
Flour Tortillas
Your Favorite Taco Toppings

Slow Cooker Pasta Fagioli Soup

Ingredients: *Serves 6-8*

1 tablespoon olive oil

1 pound spicy italian sausage

1 medium onion, chopped

2 cloves garlic, minced

1 (14.5-oz) can diced tomatoes with juices

1 stalk celery, diced

1 tablespoon oregano

2 teaspoons basil

6 cups chicken stock (homemade page 113)

1 (16-oz.) can white kidney beans, drained

1 cup small shell pasta

parmesan cheese

Directions:

1. In a skillet, heat olive oil.
2. Add sausage, cook and crumble until no longer pink.
3. Add cooked sausage along with all remaining ingredients except pasta and parmesan to slow cooker.
4. Cook on low 6-7 hours or high for 3-4 hours. Add uncooked pasta and continue to cook for an additional 1 hour or until pasta is cooked.
5. Serve in individual bowls with a sprinkle of parmesan cheese.

Monthly Shopping List

		Weekly Shopping List
Olive Oil	Spicy Ital. Sausage (freeze)	Onion
Diced Tomatoes	Oregano	Garlic
Basil	Chicken Stock	Celery
White Kidney Beans	Shell Pasta	Parmesan Cheese

Chapter 10

Mixes & Sauces

Homemade mixes and sauces can be lifesavers when it comes to preparing quick and easy meals. As an added bonus, you won't worry about sodium or preservatives because you're in control of the ingredients!

Onion Soup Mix

Perfect for recipes that call for onion soup mix. You'll find it handy for all kinds of roasts, soups and slow cooker recipes.

Ingredients:

> 4 teaspoons beef bouillion
> 8 teaspoons dried onion flakes
> 1 teaspoon onion powder
> 1/4 teaspoon garlic powder

Directions:

1. Combine all ingredients.
2. Store in an airtight container for up to one year away from moisture.

Sloppy Joe Seasoning

Ingredients:

2 cups chili powder

1/4 cup paprika

3 tablespoons dry ground mustard

1 tablespoon cumin

1 tablespoon onion powder

1 tablespoon salt

2 teaspoons garlic powder

5 teaspoons beef bouillon

2 teaspoons pepper

Directions:

1. Combine all ingredients and store in an airtight container away from moisture. Keeps for up to one year.
2. To make sloppy joes: combine 2 tablespoon Sloppy Joe Seasoning with 1 pound of ground beef (cooked and drained), along with 3/4 cup ketchup.

Cream of _____ Soup Alternative

Looking for a healthier alternative for recipes calling for cream soup? Here's a dry mix you can keep in your pantry until you need it.

Ingredients:

2 cups powdered nonfat dry milk

3/4 cup cornstarch

1/4 cup chicken bouillon granules

1 teaspoon dried thyme

1 teaspoon dried basil

1 teaspoon onion powder

1/2 teaspoon pepper

Directions:

Mix well and store in airtight container.

Cream of Chicken Soup Alternative:

Use 1/3 cup mix with 1¼ cup water for the equivalent of one can. Whisk until combined. Cook on stovetop over medium heat until thickened, stirring often.

Cream of Mushroom Soup Alternative:

Use 1/3 cup mix with 1¼ cup water for the equivalent of one can. Whisk until combined. Add 1/2 cup fresh mushrooms. Cook on stovetop over medium heat until thickened, stirring often.

Cream of Celery Soup Alternative:

Follow instructions for Cream of Mushroom Soup Alternative, substituting 1/2 cup chopped celery for mushrooms.

Cream of Broccoli Soup Alternative:

Follow instructions for Cream of Mushroom Soup Alternative, substituting 1/2 cup chopped broccoli for mushrooms.

Italian Dressing Mix

Ingredients:

4 tablespoons salt

2 tablespoons oregano

2 tablespoons parsley

2 tablespoons sugar

2 tablespoons garlic salt

2 tablespoons onion powder

2 teaspoons fresh cracked black pepper

1/2 teaspoon basil

1/2 teaspoon celery salt

Directions:

1. Mix all ingredients and store in airtight container for up to one year.
2. To make salad dressing: add 2 tablespoons dressing mix, 1/4 cup vinegar, 3 tablespoons water, and 1/2 cup vegetable oil or olive oil. Shake well and serve.

Taco Seasoning Mix

Ingredients:

2 teaspoons chili powder

1½ teaspoons ground cumin

1 teaspoon cornstarch

1 teaspoon beef bouillon granules

1/2 teaspoon garlic powder

1/4 teaspoon onion powder

1/2 teaspoon paprika

1/2 teaspoon salt

1 teaspoon black pepper

1/4 teaspoon dried oregano

1/4 teaspoon crushed red pepper flakes

Directions:

1. Mix together and store in airtight container for up to one year.
2. To make tacos: add 1 lb. cooked ground beef and 1/3 cup water per 2 tablespoons taco seasoning. Simmer uncovered on low for 5-10 minutes.

Ranch Dressing Mix

Ingredients:

> 1/2 cup powdered buttermilk
> 2 tablespoon dried parsley
> 2 teaspoons onion powder
> 1 teaspoon dried dill weed
> 1/2 teaspoon salt
> 1/2 teaspoon garlic powder
> 1/4 teaspoon ground pepper

Directions:

1. Combine all ingredients in a blender to create a fine consistency. Store in an airtight container for up to one year.
2. To make ranch dressing: mix one tablespoon dressing mix with one cup whole milk and one cup mayo. Use less mayo if you like a thinner consistency, more if you like it thick.

Cornbread Mix

Ingredients:

> 4 cups flour
> 2 cups yellow cornmeal
> 1 cup granulated sugar
> 1/3 cup baking powder
> 1 1/2 teaspoon salt

Directions:

1. Combine all ingredients in a large bowl.
2. Store in an airtight container for up to 10 weeks.

To Make Cornbread:
1. Combine 1 ¼ cup cornbread mix with 1 egg, 1/3 cup milk and two tablespoons vegetable oil.
2. Pour into a greased 8x8" inch pan. Bake at 425°F for 18-20 minutes.

To Make Cornbread Muffins:
1. Combine 1 ¼ cup cornbread mix with 1 egg, 1/3 cup milk and two tablespoons vegetable oil.
2. Fill a greased muffin pan half full. Bake at 400°F for 15-20 minutes. Makes 6 muffins.

Basic Baking Mix

Use this in place of store bought all-purpose baking mix to make biscuits, pizza crust, pot pies and lots more.

Ingredients:

> 8 cups flour
> 1 1/2 cups instant nonfat dry milk
> 1/3 cup baking powder
> 2 tablespoons cream of tartar
> 2 cups vegetable shortening

Directions:

1. In a large bowl mix together first four ingredients.
2. Cut in vegetable shortening until thoroughly combined.
3. Store in an airtight container for up to 6 months.

To Make Biscuits:

> Mix together 2 cups baking mix and 1/3 to 1/2 cup water. Drop by spoonful onto greased baking sheet. Bake at 450°F for 10-12 minutes.

To Make Soda Biscuits:

> Combine 2 cups baking mix 1/2 cup sour cream. Then add 1/2 cup lemon lime soda. Cut dough into 9 equal pieces and place on an 8x8" baking sheet. Drizzle with 1/4 cup melted butter. Bake at 450°F for 12-15 minutes.

To Make Fruit Cobbler:

> Combine 2 ¼ cup baking mix with 1/4 cup sugar, 1/4 cup melted butter and 1/2 cup milk. Layer your favorite sweetened fruit on the bottom of a greased 8x8" pan, adding baking mixture on top. Sprinkle lightly with cinnamon & sugar. Bake at 350°F for 30-45 minutes or until golden brown.

Pancake and Waffle Mix

Looking for ways to use up your frozen fruit or yummy blueberry syrup from page 107? Well your search is over. This delicious pancake mix will have you out the door in no time in the morning with a full and happy tummy.

Ingredients:

> 3 1/2 cups all-purpose flour
>
> 4 teaspoons baking powder
>
> 2 teaspoons baking soda
>
> 1 teaspoon salt
>
> 1/4 cup granulated sugar

Directions:

1. Combine all ingredients in a large bowl.
2. Store in an airtight container for up to 6 months and makes 6-7 batches.

To Make Pancakes:
1. Combine 2 cups pancake mix with 2 eggs, 2 tablespoons melted butter, 1 cup whole milk, 1 cup buttermilk and 1 teaspoon vanilla. Whisk together.
2. Pour batter onto hot greased griddle. Flip when bubbles form around the sides and top. Continue to cook until second side is golden brown. Makes 6-8 pancakes.

To Make Waffles:
1. Combine 2 cups mix with 2 eggs, 2 tablespoons melted butter, 2 cups buttermilk and 2 teaspoons vanilla. Whisk together.
2. Makes 6-8 waffles.

Brownie Mix

Ingredients:

> 6 cups all-purpose flour
>
> 8 cups sugar
>
> 1 (8-oz) box unsweetened cocoa powder
>
> 4 teaspoons baking powder
>
> 1 tablespoon salt

Directions:

1. Combine all ingredients in a large bowl.
2. Store in an airtight container for up to 3 months.

To Make Brownies:
1. Mix together 2 ¼ cups brownie mix with 2 eggs, 1/4 cup softened butter and 1 teaspoon vanilla.
2. Pour into greased 8x8" pan and bake at 350°F for 30 minutes.

Graham Cracker Crust Mix

Ingredients:

> 1 (2 lb.) box graham crackers
> 1 cup granulated sugar

Directions:

1. Grind crackers into fine crumbs using a blender or food processor. Mix well with sugar.
2. Store in an airtight container for up to 6 months.

To Make Graham Cracker Crust:

1. Mix 1 ½ cups graham cracker crust mix with 1/3 cup melted butter.
2. Press into pie dish.
3. Refrigerate for at least 30 minutes before filling.

Freezer Friendly Pasta Sauce

Ingredients:

2 28 oz. cans whole tomatoes or 20 fresh tomatoes, peels removed

1 6 oz. can tomato paste

1 medium onion, diced

6 cloves garlic, minced

2 teaspoons kosher salt

1/2 cup chicken stock (homemade page 113)

1 tablespoon olive oil

1 teaspoon pepper

1 teaspoon red pepper flakes

2 teaspoons sugar

2 teaspoons dried parsley flakes

1 teaspoon dried basil

Directions:

1. Heat olive oil in a large saucepan. Add onions and cook until translucent.
2. On a cutting board, make a paste out of minced garlic and kosher salt. Add it to the pan and cook for 1-2 minutes.
3. Add chicken stock and stir.
4. Crush whole tomatoes with a handheld mixer to desired consistency and add to pan.
5. Add tomato paste, pepper, red pepper flakes and sugar. Simmer for 1-2 hours.
6. Add parsley and basil and continue cooking for 10 minutes.
7. Store in a freezer safe container in meal size portions of approximately 3-5 cups depending on your family size. This recipe will make 2-3 meals.

TIP: Want to avoid the hassle of peeling your tomatoes? Freeze them! Once thawed, the skins will slip right off under running water. See page 101 for details.

Freezer Friendly Pizza Sauce

Ingredients:

2 (14.5 oz.) cans stewed tomatoes or 10 fresh tomatoes, peels removed

1 (6 oz.) can tomato paste

1/2 cup chicken stock (homemade page 113)

4 tablespoons chopped fresh parsley

1 clove garlic, minced

1 teaspoon dried oregano

1 teaspoon salt

1/4 teaspoon fresh ground black pepper

6 tablespoons olive oil

Directions:
1. Process all ingredients in a food processor.
2. Freeze in 5-10 individual bags for up to 3 months. Thaw as needed!
3. If you plan to use some immediately, it is best to allow the flavors to marry for at least 1-2 hours before serving.

Index

Manufactured by Amazon.ca
Bolton, ON